Network Scanning Cookbook

Practical network security using Nmap and Nessus 7

Sairam Jetty

BIRMINGHAM - MUMBAI

Network Scanning Cookbook

Commissioning Editor: Pavan Ramchandani
Acquisition Editor: Akshay Jethani
Content Development Editor: Nithin George Varghese
Technical Editor: Komal Karne
Copy Editor: Safis Editing
Project Coordinator: Drashti Panchal
Proofreader: Safis Editing
Indexer: Priyanka Dhadke
Graphics: Tom Scaria
Production Coordinator: Aparna Bhagat

First published: September 2018

Production reference: 1290918

Published by Packt Publishing Ltd.
Livery Place
35 Livery Street
Birmingham
B3 2PB, UK.

ISBN 978-1-78934-648-0

www.packtpub.com

`mapt.io`

Mapt is an online digital library that gives you full access to over 5,000 books and videos, as well as industry leading tools to help you plan your personal development and advance your career. For more information, please visit our website.

Why subscribe?

- Spend less time learning and more time coding with practical eBooks and Videos from over 4,000 industry professionals

- Improve your learning with Skill Plans built especially for you

- Get a free eBook or video every month

- Mapt is fully searchable

- Copy and paste, print, and bookmark content

Packt.com

Did you know that Packt offers eBook versions of every book published, with PDF and ePub files available? You can upgrade to the eBook version at `www.packt.com` and as a print book customer, you are entitled to a discount on the eBook copy. Get in touch with us at `customercare@packtpub.com` for more details.

At `www.packt.com`, you can also read a collection of free technical articles, sign up for a range of free newsletters, and receive exclusive discounts and offers on Packt books and eBooks.

Foreword

Nessus and Nmap are among the most useful tools that a pentester relies on. However, it is difficult to find detailed information on how to use these tools and their rich set of features. This book covers all such aspects, ranging right from installation to configuration and execution. This book will help you gain mastery over some of the lesser known but very handy features of these tools, including how to use Nmap in a network with high latency and how to perform time-throttled scanning.

The book includes several real-life scenarios encountered by the author as part of his numerous ethical hacking assignments, making the content relevant and insightful for first-time users looking to gain confidence as well as those who are perhaps more seasoned.

If you are looking to master compliance scanning using Nessus and want to tweak things to meet your custom requirements, look no further—this book will help you understand this feature in detail and make the best of it. Another feature that would be of interest to security enthusiasts and that is covered in this book, is Nmap custom scripting, which is indispensable for when you want to create scripts where official scripts are not available.

Several such features are covered in the experience that the author shares with you, and they will not only help you understand the need for such advanced tools and capabilities, but will also equip you with what you need to master them.

Sairam is a veteran in the network and application security testing domain. With more than 5 years' experience in executing security projects for enterprise customers across the globe, he has really pushed the limits when it comes to use of the domain's tools. I am sure that you will gain a number of insights into the use of these tools and the real-world scenarios where each of these features can be applied.

Jose Varghese
EVP & HEAD – MDR SERVICES, Co-Founder – Paladion Networks Pvt Ltd.

Contributors

About the author

Sairam Jetty has more than 5 years of hands-on experience in many verticals of penetration testing, compliance, digital forensics, and malware research, and is currently working with Paladion Networks, Abu Dhabi, as a senior analyst and team lead. He has been assisting and associated with various financial, telecom, and industrial institutions with regard to testing and securing their applications and environments. Sairam has industry-standard certifications, such as OSCP, Digital Forensic Analyst, Digital Forensic Investigator, and Mobile Security Expert. He also specializes in source code review and mobile application security. He has acquired a great deal of knowledge of SCADA/ICS and nuclear security from his corporate experience and self-learning.

I would like to thank my family for being my strength. Thanks to Prashant Verma and Dinesh Barai for their technical support. Thanks to the team at Packt for the support they have extended, and special thanks to Nithin George Varghese and Akshay Jethani for putting up with me.

About the reviewer

Prashant Verma (CISSP, QSA) leads the Incidence Response, Digital Forensics, and Red Team operations at Paladion Networks. He loves to evangelize about detection and response engineering. He has a strong background in vulnerability management and security auditing. He is co-author of *Mobile Device Exploitation Cookbook* and *Security Testing Handbook for Banking Applications*. He has presented at security conferences such as RSA, OWASP, NIBM, ISACA, and ClubHack. He has also authored security articles and given guest lectures and security training on a number of occasions.

Packt is searching for authors like you

If you're interested in becoming an author for Packt, please visit `authors.packtpub.com` and apply today. We have worked with thousands of developers and tech professionals, just like you, to help them share their insight with the global tech community. You can make a general application, apply for a specific hot topic that we are recruiting an author for, or submit your own idea.

Table of Contents

Preface

Network Scanning Cookbook is intended for the intermediate and advanced audience in the field of information security. This book enables a user to understand the key aspects of network security scanning using Nmap and Nessus. It begins with an introduction to network scanning techniques and quickly moves onto the specifics of using Nmap and Nessus to perform network scans for configuration audits of devices. This book also explores a number of tools that will make your network scanning techniques highly customizable, further catering to the needs of any complex network audits that you might have to carry out. The book ends by looking at how these tools can be used to perform simple audits on critical systems such as SCADA/ICS.

Who this book is for

This book acts as a great resource for network administrators trying to identify their network security posture, beginners in information security who are looking to leap into their information security careers, and executives such as information security consultants and information security auditors.

What this book covers

Chapter 1, *Introduction to Network Vulnerability Scanning*, introduces basic network components and their architecture. It also explains the methods and methodologies of network vulnerability scanning and the complexities involved in it, and looks at mitigation planning for identified vulnerabilities.

Chapter 2, *Understanding Network Scanning Tools*, consists of recipes that will give you a basic understanding of the Nessus and Nmap tools, including the technical requirements to install these tools and the details of their workings. The chapter then dives into the installation and removal instructions for Nessus and Nmap.

Chapter 3, *Port Scanning*, consists of recipes on techniques for performing port scanning. It begins with instructions and details regarding host discovery, moving to open ports, scripts, and version scanning. It also gives insights into evading network protection systems while performing port scans.

Chapter 4, *Vulnerability Scanning*, consists of recipes on managing the features of Nessus, such as policies, settings, and user accounts. You will also get get to grips with the steps for performing a network vulnerability scan using Nessus before then managing the scan results.

Chapter 5, *Configuration Audit*, consists of recipes for performing configuration audits and gap analyses on multiple platforms using Nessus. It takes you through a step-by-step process for creating, selecting, and configuring policies to perform configuration audits on operating systems, databases, and web applications.

Chapter 6, *Report Analysis and Confirmation*, will teach you how to create effective reports by analyzing the results from Nmap and Nessus scans. The recipes in this chapter will give a detailed insight into the supported report types and the level of customization these tools allow. It also gives details on some techniques for confirming vulnerabilities reported by Nessus and Nmap using various tools.

Chapter 7, *Understanding the Customization and Optimization of Nessus and Nmap*, teaches you about the creation of custom scripts and audit files for Nmap and Nessus. These recipes provide step-by-step procedures for replicating the method for the customization of audit files.

Chapter 8, *Network Scanning for IoT, SCADA, and ICS*, consists of recipes for understanding the network scanning procedure for SCADA and ICS systems. The recipes outline methods for using Nmap and Nessus to perform port scanning and network vulnerability scanning by ensuring the high availability of these critical systems.

To get the most out of this book

You should have a good working knowledge of computer networks and vulnerability scanning so you can understand the terminologies and methodologies used in this book.

In order to follow the recipes, you will need to be running Windows or Kali Linux, and will require Metasploitable 2 by Rapid7 with the latest versions of Nmap and Nessus. For some of the recipes, such as those to do with configuration audits, you will need to have a Nessus professional license.

Download the color images

We also provide a PDF file that has color images of the screenshots/diagrams used in this book. You can download it here: `https://www.packtpub.com/sites/default/files/downloads/9781789346480_ColorImages.pdf`.

Conventions used

There are a number of text conventions used throughout this book.

`CodeInText`: Indicates code words in text, database table names, folder names, filenames, file extensions, pathnames, dummy URLs, user input, and Twitter handles. Here is an example: "Install the downloaded `.msi` file by following the instructions."

Any command-line input or output is written as follows:

```
nmap -sS -sV -PN -T4 -oA testsmtp -p T:25 -v -r 192.168.1.*
```

Bold: Indicates a new term, an important word, or words that you see on screen. For example, words in menus or dialog boxes appear in the text like this. Here is an example: "Select **Quick scan** from the **Profile** drop-down list."

 Warnings or important notes appear like this.

 Tips and tricks appear like this.

Sections

In this book, you will find several headings that appear frequently (*Getting ready*, *How to do it...*, *How it works...*, *There's more...*, and *See also*).

To give clear instructions on how to complete a recipe, use these sections as follows:

Getting ready

This section tells you what to expect in the recipe and describes how to set up any software or any preliminary settings required for the recipe.

How to do it...

This section contains the steps required to follow the recipe.

How it works...

This section usually consists of a detailed explanation of what happened in the previous section.

There's more...

This section consists of additional information about the recipe in order to make you more knowledgeable about the recipe.

See also

This section provides helpful links to other useful information for the recipe.

Get in touch

Feedback from our readers is always welcome.

General feedback: If you have questions about any aspect of this book, mention the book title in the subject of your message and email us at `customercare@packtpub.com`.

Errata: Although we have taken every care to ensure the accuracy of our content, mistakes do happen. If you have found a mistake in this book, we would be grateful if you would report this to us. Please visit `www.packt.com/submit-errata`, selecting your book, clicking on the Errata Submission Form link, and entering the details.

Piracy: If you come across any illegal copies of our works in any form on the internet, we would be grateful if you would provide us with the location address or website name. Please contact us at copyright@packt.com with a link to the material.

If you are interested in becoming an author: If there is a topic that you have expertise in and you are interested in either writing or contributing to a book, please visit authors.packtpub.com.

Reviews

Please leave a review. Once you have read and used this book, why not leave a review on the site that you purchased it from? Potential readers can then see and use your unbiased opinion to make purchase decisions, we at Packt can understand what you think about our products, and our authors can see your feedback on their book. Thank you!

For more information about Packt, please visit packt.com.

1
Introduction to Network Vulnerability Scanning

In today's times, where hackers are prevalent and there are critical vulnerabilities discovered in various products every day, corporate networks are required to create procedures to identify, analyze, and mitigate vulnerabilities in real time. In this cookbook, we will be looking into various procedures and tools required to perform network security scanning and to understand and act on the results obtained.

This cookbook will equip any reader with a basic knowledge of computer networks with recipes to prepare, plan, and execute a Network Vulnerability Scan and determine the targets for a penetration test, or just to understand the security posture of the network. This will help budding penetration testers to conquer and learn to cook their methods to perform preliminary steps to identify vulnerabilities.

This chapter will introduce you to the basics of computer networks. It also dives into the procedures, uses, and various complexities to consider while performing a Network Vulnerability Scan. This chapter will equip you with basic knowledge of how to plan a Network Vulnerability Scan.

In this chapter, we will cover the following:

- Basic networks and their components
- Network Vulnerability Scanning
- Flow of procedures used in Network Vulnerability Scanning
- Uses of performing a Network Vulnerability Scan
- Complexity of performing network scans
- How to devise a mitigation plan and respond

Basic networks and their components

A basic corporate network typically consists of endpoints such as desktops/laptops, servers, security devices such as Firewall, proxy, intrusion detection and prevention systems, and network devices such as hubs, switches, and routers. Most of the time, these are acquired from various vendors, thus they are susceptible to different attacks, and expose the network to a larger attack surface. These components can be attacked by a hacker using publicly available exploits or a zero-day vulnerability to gain access to the device/machine with a possibility of gaining access to a different device/machine in the network or whole network itself. Note the following diagram to illustrate this:

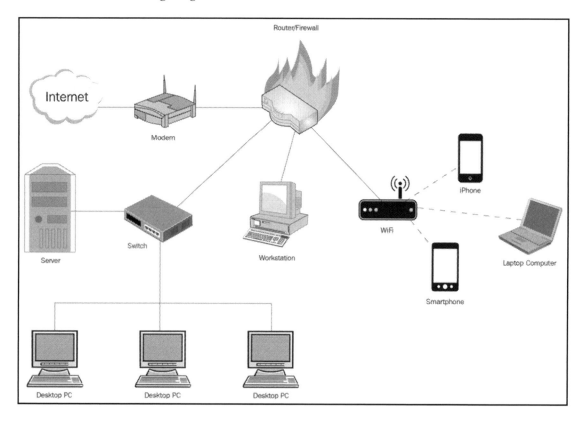

Network Vulnerability Scanning

A vulnerability is a weakness present in a system or device that is exposed to a possibility of being attacked. Network Vulnerability Scanning is a process of looking into identifying and detecting vulnerabilities in the network components such as clients, servers, network devices, and endpoints, using various automated or manual tools and techniques. It can be broadly classified into two types: internal network vulnerability scan and external network vulnerability scan.

The internal and external vulnerability scans share a similar process, but differ in the network placement of the scan appliance or the system. An external vulnerability scan has a scope to identify loopholes with a perspective of the attacker being over the internet and targeting the network through public IP addresses of the network, whereas an internal vulnerability scan operates considering the attacker to be an insider with access to the internal network and targeting the network through private IP addresses. Identifying both internal and external threats is very important for any computer network, to create a real-time picture of how secure the network is, based on the number of vulnerabilities identified.

The vulnerability scans have their own side effects on the networks, such as an increase in network latency caused by the increase in traffic, unresponsive network resources, and rebooting of devices and servers. Thus, all internal network scans within the organization should be performed with the utmost care and proper approvals. In general, there are two types of scanning techniques that can be used, authenticated and unauthenticated. We will see the recipes for these scan types in `Chapter 4`, *Vulnerability Scanning*, and `Chapter 5`, *Configuration Audit*.

Beginners always confuse the Vulnerability Scan with the penetration test. The Vulnerability Scan is a preliminary step to identify the hosts on which you can perform a penetration test. For example, as a part of a vulnerability scan you identify that port 80 is open on a server and is susceptible to **Remote Code Execution (RCE)** attacks. For a penetration test, this information will be input as you already know that the server is vulnerable to RCE and will try to perform the attack and compromise the server.

 Before performing a Network Vulnerability Scan, it is always recommended to inform the stakeholders and obtain downtime if required based on how critical the servers and the data hosted on the servers are. It is a good practice to write an email before beginning the scan and after completion of the scan as this would help the respective teams to check the continuity of the service.

We will have a look at many recipes in further chapters of this cookbook to understand the various best practices to be followed during a Network Vulnerability Scan.

Flow of procedures

The activity of a Network Vulnerability Scan can be divided into three phases:

- Discovery
- Port scanning
- Vulnerability scanning

Discovery

Discovery, also known as **Host Discovery**, is a process to enumerate live hosts and is a very important component of the reconnaissance phase of a security testing activity. This will help you to eliminate the unwanted hosts from the list of targets, thus it will allow you to use these enumerated hosts to perform targeted scans and penetration tests. Some of the tools that can be used to perform Network Discovery are Nmap, Nessus, OpenVas, and Wireshark.

The following screenshot shows a sample host scanned using Nmap for Discovery. It shows that the host is up, thus we can determine the host is live:

```
C:\Users\admin>nmap -Pn 192.168.100.142
Starting Nmap 7.70 ( https://nmap.org ) at 2018-06-11 14:04 Arabian Standard Time
Nmap scan report for 192.168.100.142
Host is up (0.00064s latency).
All 1000 scanned ports on 192.168.100.142 are closed
MAC Address: 00:0C:29:DF:F9:77 (VMware)

Nmap done: 1 IP address (1 host up) scanned in 28.07 seconds
```

These tools come in handy if the ping is disabled across the network. I always prefer using Nmap over other tools because of its ease of use and the **Nmap Script Engine** (NSE), which allows the user to write and implement custom scripts. We will be discussing NSE in coming chapters.

In this cookbook we will further introduce you to various recipes on how to perform host discovery manually and using tools.

Port scanning

In this phase, we will perform detection of the ports open for a specific host based on the communication between the host on that port to your machine. This technique helps to determine whether a particular port is open or closed. This technique differs from protocol to protocol. For example, for TCP, the communication and the pattern to conclude a port to be open is different when compared to UDP. Some of the tools that can be used to perform port scanning are Nmap, Nessus, OpenVas, and Wireshark.

The following screenshot shows a sample host scanned using Nmap for port 80. The screenshot shows that the host is up and port 80 with state as open, thus we can determine the host is live. These tools come in handy if the ping is disabled across the network:

```
C:\Users\admin>nmap -sS -Pn -p80 192.168.100.143
Starting Nmap 7.70 ( https://nmap.org ) at 2018-06-11 14:29 Arabian Standard Time
Nmap scan report for 192.168.100.143
Host is up (0.00s latency).

PORT     STATE SERVICE
80/tcp open   http
MAC Address: 00:0C:29:DF:F9:77 (VMware)

Nmap done: 1 IP address (1 host up) scanned in 27.77 seconds
```

In this cookbook, we will further introduce you to various recipes on how to perform port scanning manually and using tools.

Vulnerability scanning

Once the open ports are identified on the discovered live hosts, we can perform vulnerability scanning. A vulnerability scan detects and identifies known issues of the software and tools installed on a host such as older version of software in use, vulnerable protocols enabled, and default passwords. It is difficult to perform this activity manually; hence this phase needs to be performed using automated tools that identify the open ports and try various exploits on the ports to identify whether the particular process/software using the port is vulnerable to the exploit based on the process. Some of the tools used to perform vulnerability scanning are Nessus, OpenVas, and Qualys.

The following screenshot shows a sample host scanned for vulnerabilities using OpenVas. You can see that the output shows the list of vulnerabilities the host is affected:

Vulnerability	Severity	QoD	Host	Location	Created
HTTP Server type and version	0.0 (Log)	80%	192.168.1.107	5357/tcp	Mon Jun 11 22:42:12 2018
SMB NativeLanMan	0.0 (Log)	95%	192.168.1.107	445/tcp	Mon Jun 11 22:37:31 2018
DIRB (NASL wrapper)	0.0 (Log)	80%	192.168.1.107	5357/tcp	Mon Jun 11 22:49:45 2018
DIRB (NASL wrapper)	0.0 (Log)	80%	192.168.1.107	2869/tcp	Mon Jun 11 22:49:45 2018
DIRB (NASL wrapper)	0.0 (Log)	80%	192.168.1.107	443/tcp	Mon Jun 11 22:49:48 2018
DIRB (NASL wrapper)	0.0 (Log)	80%	192.168.1.107	443/tcp	Mon Jun 11 22:49:48 2018
SSL/TLS: Certificate - Self-Signed Certificate Detection	0.0 (Log)	98%	192.168.1.107	443/tcp	Mon Jun 11 22:47:07 2018

1 - 10 of 26

In this cookbook, we will further introduce you to various recipes on how to scan a host for vulnerabilities using Nessus, and how to customize these scans to obtain specific and fewer false-positive results.

Uses

As mentioned in the earlier sections of the chapter, the major advantage of performing a Network Vulnerability Scan is to understand the security posture of the network. The result of a Network Vulnerability Scan provides a bundle of information useful to both administrators and penetration testers, such as the following:

- Unwanted ports are open and services running
- Default user account and password information
- Missing patches, updates, and upgrades
- Vulnerable version of software installed
- Vulnerable protocols in use
- Vulnerable algorithms in use
- Exploit information for all the preceding vulnerabilities

The Network Vulnerability Scan allows the identification of unnecessary ports that are open and the services running on these ports. For example, an application/web server in a demilitarized zone does not require TCP port 22 to be open and exposed to the internet. These unwanted ports make the host/device susceptible to attacks. Most of the scanners, when identifying a login interface to any of the hosted services, try to log in using a preexisting database of usernames and passwords, and provide a report of all the default usernames and passwords, the use of which can compromise the service.

A credentialed patch scan can reveal details about missing patches and updates for a variety of supported platforms. This information is critical as most of these missing patches have exploits available over the internet, which can be made use of to reproduce similar attacks on the network. This might also reveal various missing patches in the third-party tools installed on the machines of the network. This information helps an attacker to target these tools to exploit and obtain access to the nodes or, sometimes, even the entire network.

A Network Vulnerability Scan also highlights various vulnerable protocols used within the network or on the nodes. For example, if a server is running an SMB share supporting the SMBv1 protocol, it will be highlighted as vulnerability with an above moderate risk rating as SMBv1 is vulnerable to various known malware attacks. Also, a scan highlights the vulnerable ciphers and authentication methods used by the services running which are susceptible to known Man-in-the-Middle attacks. For example, if a web server is using basic authentication over HTTP protocol, it is vulnerable to expose user credentials when a Man-in-the-Middle attack is performed on the network.

Most of the vulnerability scanners, both open source and paid software, provide attack-related exploit information as a part of the description of the vulnerability. This will make the life of the attacker and the penetration tester easy by providing direct links either to the method of exploitation or the exploit code itself.

The following screenshot provides links to documents providing information about the vulnerability reported by the scanner:

Log Method
Details: Check for SMB accessible registry (OID: 1.3.6.1.4.1.25623.1.0.10400)

Version used: $Revision: 7186 $

References

Other: http://docs.greenbone.net/GSM-Manual/gos-3.1/en/scanning.html#requirements-on-target-systems-with-windows

http://docs.greenbone.net/GSM-Manual/gos-4/en/vulnerabilitymanagement.html#requirements-on-target-systems-with-windows

Along with the previous technical use cases, a network vulnerability also has various uses from an organization's perspective, such as the following:

- Giving importance and bringing focus to information security
- Helping to find potential risks proactively
- Resulting in network update
- Advancing development in the administrative knowledge
- Preventing financial loss in critical infrastructures
- Prioritizing the vulnerabilities that require escalated patching versus delayed patching

Complexity

Today's network environments have a complex structure consisting of firewalls, DMZ, and network devices such as switches and routers. These devices consist of complex access lists and virtual network configurations, which makes it difficult to generalize any activity. A shift in any of the preceding configurations could result in a change of the architecture of the whole network.

If we are looking to perform an IP-based scan on any of the network components, we have to be sure that all the data packets generated are reaching the destination intact and are not being impacted by any of the devices or solutions in between. For example, if Alice is scanning Bob's computer over the network and both of them are separated by a firewall, where Bob's subnet is configured to be in WAN Ping Block Mode as a part of which ping packets will be identified and dropped at the firewall level, Alice's host discovery scans for Bob's computer will result in a false positive that machine is not live.

In order to perform a successful security profiling using a Network Vulnerability Scan, the following factors need to be considered:

- Scope of the scan
- Network architecture
- Network access

Scope of the scan

If we are required to perform a vulnerability assessment for a specific application's infrastructure, it is very important to identify the data transmission sources and the components involved in the end-to-end communication. This will allow the penetration tester to perform the vulnerability scan on this scope and identify vulnerabilities specific to this application. Instead, if we choose to scan the subnets or a broader range of IP addresses, we might end up highlighting unnecessary vulnerabilities, which most of the time leads to confusion during the remediation phase. For example, if we are looking to audit a web-based application, we might be looking to include a web application, application server, web server, and database server as part of the audit scope.

Network architecture

It is always important to understand the placement of the IP address or the component on which we are performing vulnerability scanning. This will help us to customize our approach and to reduce false positives. For example, if Alice is trying to scan a web application hosted behind a web application firewall, she needs to customize the payloads or the scripts used to identify vulnerabilities using techniques such as encoding, to ensure that the payloads are not blocked by the web application firewall.

Network access

When tasked to perform Network Vulnerability Scans on a huge network, it is very important to know whether proper access has been provided to your appliance or host to perform the scanning activity. A network vulnerability scan performed without proper network access will yield incomplete results. It is always recommended to have the scanner appliance or host IP address to be whitelisted across the network devices to obtain full access to the scope of the scan.

Response

Once a Network Vulnerability Scan report is obtained, it is important to devise a mitigation plan to mitigate all the vulnerabilities highlighted as part of the report. The following are a few solutions that can be part of the Network Security Scan report:

- Close unwanted ports and disable unwanted services
- Use strong and uncommon passwords
- Always apply latest patches and updates
- Uninstall or update older versions of software
- Disable legacy and old protocols in use
- Use strong algorithms and authentication mechanism

The report needs to be compiled based on the findings, and tasks are to be assigned to the respective departments. For example, all the Windows-related vulnerabilities are to be mitigated by the respective team that is responsible for maintaining Windows machines. Once the responsibilities have been sorted across the teams, the teams are expected to perform an impact and feasibility analysis on the solution provided in the report. The teams have to check the solutions against the security objectives, confidentiality, integrity, and availability. These mitigations can be used as a baseline to create hardening documents, including any other available baselines in public or private domains.

Once the solutions have been implemented on the affected hosts, it is important for the team to include these recommended remediations into the existing policies in order to avoid misconfiguration in the future. These policies are to be updated from time to time in order to be in line with the current security standards.

Any organization or individual needs to comply and create a cycle of the following activities to achieve its information security objective:

1. Vulnerability assessment
2. Mitigation analysis
3. Patch, update, and mitigate

A vulnerability assessment as mentioned previously will result in all the open gaps present in the network, after which mitigation analysis is required to understand the remediations that must be implemented and also to perform a feasibility check on whether it would have any impact on the continuity of the network components. Once all the remediations have been identified, implement the remediations and jump to step 1. This cycle, if performed quarterly, could ensure maximum protection to your network.

Always make sure that the solutions have been implemented on a test environment for any effects on the continuity of the applications hosted on the networks; also look for any dependencies to ensure that the network functionality is not affected.

Summary

To conclude, a Network Vulnerability Scan is a three-phase process including discovery, port scanning, and vulnerability scanning. This, if performed correctly, will help an organization to identify its current security posture and create actionable solutions in order to improve this posture. We have seen the steps to plan a Network Vulnerability Scan in this chapter and the various factors that are involved. In further chapters, we will look into the tutorials on how to perform this Network Vulnerability Scan to identify the vulnerabilities and act on them.

2
Understanding Network Scanning Tools

In this chapter, we will cover the following:

- Introducing Nessus and Nmap
- Installing and activating Nessus
- Downloading and installing Nmap
- Updating Nessus
- Updating Nmap
- Removing Nessus
- Removing Nmap

Introducing Nessus and Nmap

In this section, we will learn about the various features available in Nmap and Nessus. This helps the user to fully understand the tools and their capabilities before using them.

Useful features of Nessus

The default screen on the Nessus web interface, **Scans**, is shown in the following screenshot; this is where you can see all the scans that you have scheduled/performed. In the top right, you can toggle between the **Scans** and **Settings** pages. Next, we will look into the scans interface:

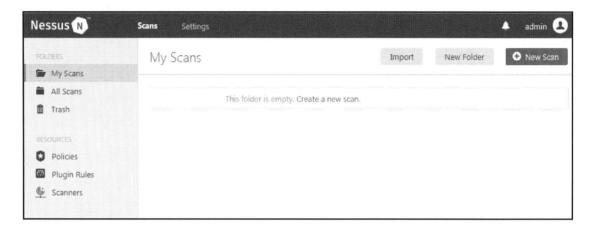

The left pane of the Nessus default screen displays multiple tabs classified into folders and resources. The folders are basically different views of scans present on the server. For example, selecting the **Trash** shows the scans that have been deleted by the user. You can further clear the trash by selecting the **Clear trash** option at the top right of the Trash folder.

Resources are one of the most important options, on the basis of which Nessus runs its scans. There are three options visible in the resources pane:

- **Policies**
- **Plugin Rules**
- **Scanners**

Policies

In order to perform a Nessus scan, you will have to create a policy. A policy is a collection of various configurations, methods, and types of scans being performed. Multiple scans can use one policy, but only one policy applies per scan. A user can import a previously created policy, which is stored in the `.nessus` format, or click **Create a new policy**. Once a user chooses to create a policy, they are presented with various policy templates present in Nessus, based on the test cases to be performed on the hosts. The following are the lists of various policy templates provided by Nessus:

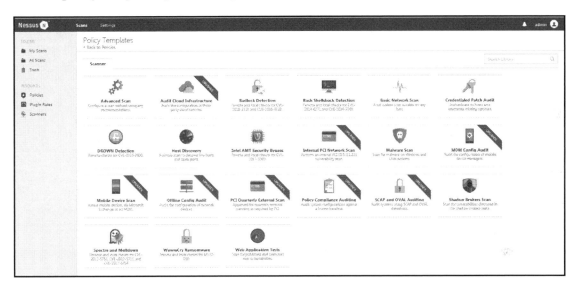

These templates consist of a range of configurations required to perform scans ranging from generic to attack specific. Out of the 21 displayed in the screenshot, we will look into a few templates to understand the composition and working of a policy.

We will look at the contents of a policy template in `Chapter 4`, *Vulnerability Scanning*.

Plugin Rules

The plugin rules allow the user to hide or change the risk rating provided by Nessus; this will allow the analyst performing a scan on large numbers of hosts to configure plugins to lower risk ratings for which they have applied workarounds. This will reduce a lot of manual efforts.

Customized Reports

This option allows the user to customize or personalize the report for a specific organization or client by uploading and adding a logo to the report:

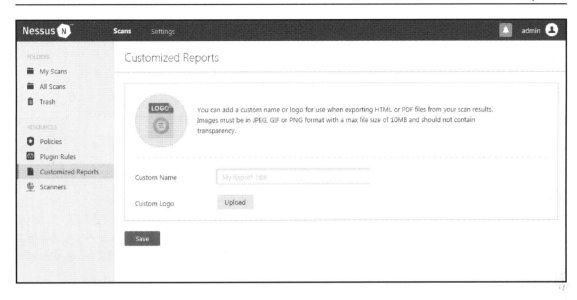

Scanners

The scanners tab displays the number of scanners available for scan and their details. Adding a scanner is not an option in Nessus Home and Professional versions, but can be added in Nessus Security Center:

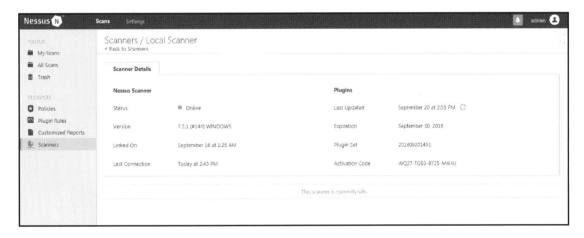

Click on the Settings to display the settings menu. Next, we will discuss the details of various options available in the settings menu.

In the preceding section, the overview tab provides a tool overview such as license information, plugin information, and so on; we will have a look at the use of the **Software Update** tab in the *Updating Nessus* recipe:

- **Master Password**: Nessus provides an option to encrypt all the scan policies and credentials used in the policies using a master password as an extra layer of protection at the file level. You can find this as part of the **Settings** menu in the web console:

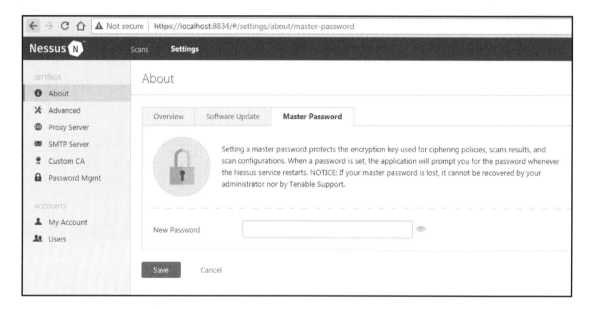

- **Proxy Server**: A proxy server is required to connect multiple networks by forwarding requests and responses without any changes. You can add a proxy server in Nessus, if you require one in your network, in order for the Nessus to reach the hosts to be scanned. You can find the **Proxy Server** option as a part of the **Settings** menu, as shown here:

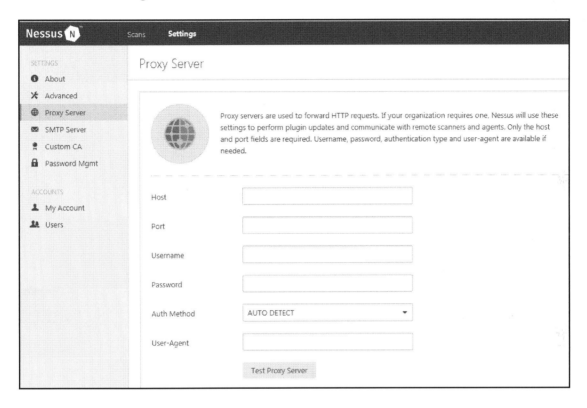

- **SMTP Server**: A **Simple Mail Transfer Protocol (SMTP)** server is required to send emails. Nessus provides the option for an email notification once the scans are complete. You can configure an SMTP server so that Nessus will be able to use this mail server to send notification emails. The SMTP configuration option can be found as a part of the settings menu, shown as follows:

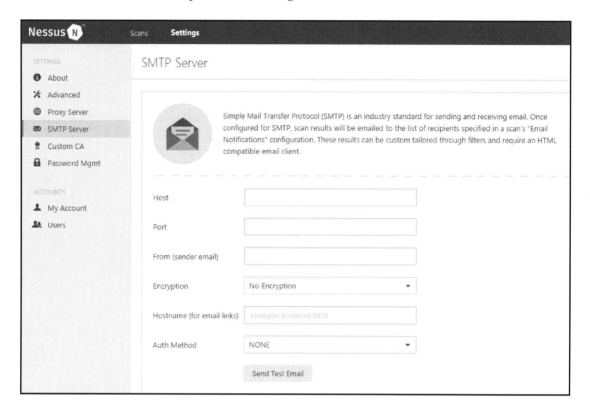

- **Custom CA**: Nessus, by default, uses a certificate signed while its installation for web based access in order for the browser to trust the certificate and negate all the certificate errors. Nessus provides an option to save a custom CA.
  The **Custom CA** option can be found as part of the **Settings** menu, shown as follows:

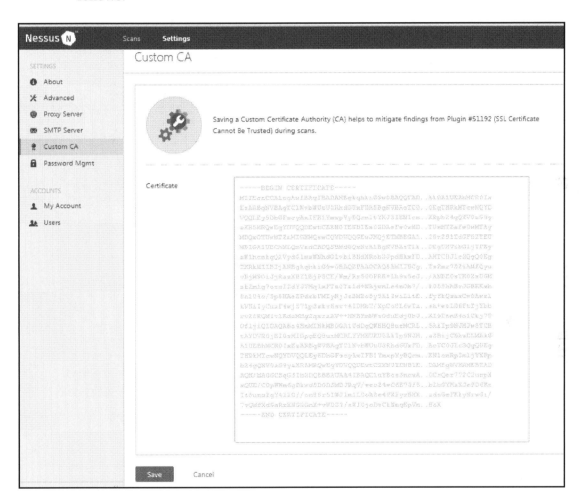

- **Password Management**: Default and weak passwords are one of the most commonly found vulnerabilities in a system, so in order to secure the Nessus console from unauthorized access, we need to configure strong passwords. For an admin to ensure strong password usage, Nessus provides a password management option with which an admin can configure parameters such as password complexity, session timeout, maximum login attempts, and minimum password length. These can be used to secure the Nessus console from password and session-related attacks. Password management options can be found in the **Settings** menu, shown as follows:

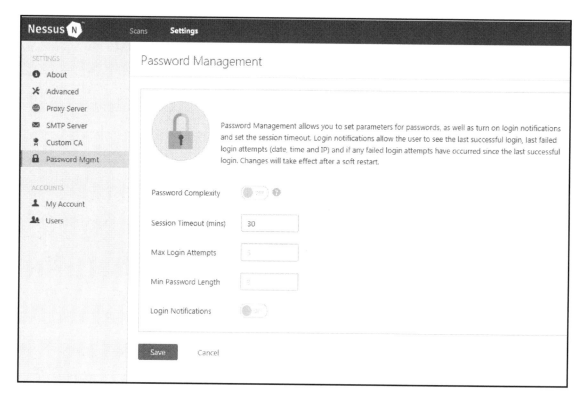

Various features of Nmap

There are various phases involved in performing a network scan using Nmap. These steps can be defined by various options provided by the Nmap utility. A user can pick any of these options, as per their requirements, to obtain specific network scan results. The following are the options provided by the Nmap utility:

- Host discovery
- Scan techniques
- Port specification and scan order
- Service or version detection
- Script scan
- OS detection
- Timing and performance
- Evasion and spoofing
- Output
- Target specification

Host discovery

A network comprises many hosts based on the subnet provided. For example, a subnet with a mask value of 27 will have 32 hosts, whereas a subnet with a mask value of 24 will have 256 hosts. A full port scan on 256 hosts, without knowing which of those hosts are live, could take a lifetime. In order to reduce the traffic generated and processed by Nmap we can filter the network hosts based on live and non-live hosts. This will allow Nmap to reduce unwanted analysis and obtain results quicker.

Scan techniques

Nmap provides various scan technique options based on the type of packets to be generated, depending on its varied nature and the protection mechanisms used in the network. These techniques construct the packet with different header values to obtain ACK or RST packets, based on which the nature of the port is decided and displayed. As mentioned earlier, some of these scan types are used to evade detection and ensure the anonymity of the user within the network.

Port specification and scan order

By default, if the range of ports to be scanned is not stipulated, Nmap scans the top 1,000 most commonly used ports, that is, ports that are found open most often across networks. These scan options allow the user to specify which ports are to be scanned and the order in which they are to be scanned.

Service or version detection

Nmap has a database of about 2,200 well-known services. Once the ports are detected to be open, these options can be used to identify the exact type and version of the service running. Nmap does this by querying these ports with specific requests and analyzes the responses received.

Script scan

Nmap has a script engine, a particularly powerful feature of the program, which allows the user to either write or use the already available scripts to perform specific tasks on the open ports by passing arguments to these scripts.

OS detection

Nmap's OS detection option helps the user to identify the operating system used by the remote host. This will help the user to further create target-specific actions and troubleshoot future compatibility issues. Nmap identifies the operating system using the TCP/UDP stack fingerprinting mechanism.

Timing and performance

Nmap provides multiple options with which a user can define multiple scan parameters pertaining to time, such as rate, timeout, and parallelism. This will allow the user to configure the scan to obtain results faster, thus increasing the performance of the scan when scanning multiple hosts and networks.

Evasion and spoofing

There are many network security solutions today, such as firewalls and IDS/IPS, which can block the network traffic generated by Nmap. Nmap provides options such as fragmentation, decoy scans, spoofing, and proxy to evade these network security solutions and successfully complete the scans and obtain results.

Output

Nmap not only is a powerful scanning tool, but also has a powerful reporting mechanism. It provides comprehensive reports in multiple formats that display output in XML and text formats.

Target specification

Nmap provides multiple target specification options with which a user can mention subnets, individual IPs, IP ranges, and IP lists to be scanned. This will allow the user to scan specific hosts identified from the host discovery.

A sample complete syntax of Nmap is as follows:

```
Nmap -sS -sV -PN -T4 -oA testsmtp -p T:25 -v -r 192.168.1.*
```

As per the user requirements, once the required options and arguments are provided, the user can perform the scan and obtain the output. We will look at recipes on how to perform network scans using Nmap in the next chapter.

As a part of this chapter, we will be covering recipes on how to choose the correct software version for both Nmap and Nessus, along with their installation and removal. These recipes are to help a new audience understand the requirements, as well as how they change from platform to platform.

Installing and activating Nessus

Nessus is a vulnerability scanner developed by Tenable Network Security. It scans hosts and subnets for network-level and service-level vulnerabilities. Nessus is available free of charge with restricted features for non-business users. It consists of two main components: NessusD (Nessus Daemon), and a client application that can be hosted on the same machine. Nessus Daemon is responsible for performing the scan and delivering the result to the client application, providing these results in various formats. Tenable also develops incremental updates and detection mechanisms, called plugins, which can be downloaded and updated regularly. It also provides additional probing functionality of known vulnerabilities; for example, if an FTP port is found to be open, Nessus will automatically try to log in using the `anonymous` user. Nessus has both a command line and web interface, but we will be mostly looking into the GUI-based web interface, due to its ease of use.

Getting ready

The requirements for Nessus vary for the different components present in it, as well as the type of license available and its usage.

The following table depicts the Nessus hardware requirements:

Scenario	Minimum recommended hardware
Nessus scanning up to 50,000 hosts	**CPU**: 4 x 2 GHz cores **Memory**: 4 GB RAM (8 GB RAM recommended) **Disk space**: 30 GB
Nessus scanning more than 50,000 hosts	**CPU**: 8 x 2 GHz cores **Memory**: 8 GB RAM (16 GB RAM recommended) **Disk space**: 30 GB (additional space may be needed for reporting)
Nessus Manager with up to 10,000 agents	**CPU**: 4 x 2 GHz cores **Memory**: 16 GB RAM **Disk space**: 30 GB (additional space may be needed for reporting)
Nessus Manager with up to 20,000 agents	**CPU**: 8 x 2 GHz cores **Memory**: 64 GB RAM **Disk space**: 30 GB (additional space may be needed for reporting)

- Nessus Agents: This is designed to consume less memory, as the process is low priority and yields to the CPU whenever asked. Nessus Agents can be installed on a virtual machine that meets the requirements specified in the following table:

Hardware	Minimum requirement
Processor	1 dual-core CPU
Processor speed	< 1 GHz
RAM	< 1 GB
Disk space	< 1 GB
Disk speed	15-50 IOPS

- Virtual machines: Nessus Agents supports the following versions of macOS, Linux, and Windows operating systems:

Operating system	Supported versions (Nessus Agents)
Linux	Debian 7, 8, and 9 - i386 Debian 7, 8, and 9 - AMD64 Red Hat ES 6/CentOS 6/Oracle Linux 6 (including Unbreakable Enterprise Kernel) - i386 Red Hat ES 6/CentOS 6/Oracle Linux 6 (including Unbreakable Enterprise Kernel) - x86_64 Red Hat ES 7/CentOS 7/Oracle Linux 7 - x86_64 Fedora 24 and 25 - x86_64 Ubuntu 12.04, 12.10, 13.04, 13.10, 14.04, and 16.04 - i386 Ubuntu 12.04, 12.10, 13.04, 13.10, 14.04, and 16.04 - AMD64
Windows	Windows 7, 8, and 10 - i386 Windows Server 2008, Server 2008 R2, Server 2012, Server 2012 R2, Server 2016, 7, 8, and 10 - x86-64
macOS X	macOS X 10.8 - 10.13

Nessus Manager supports the following versions of macOS, Linux, and Windows operating systems:

Operating System	Supported Versions (Nessus Manager)
Linux	Debian 7, 8, and 9/Kali Linux 1, 2017.1, and Rolling - i386 Debian 7, 8, and 9/Kali Linux 1, 2017.1, and Rolling - AMD64 Red Hat ES 6/CentOS 6/Oracle Linux 6 (including Unbreakable Enterprise Kernel) - i386 Red Hat ES 6/CentOS 6/Oracle Linux 6 (including Unbreakable Enterprise Kernel) - x86_64 Red Hat ES 7/CentOS 7/Oracle Linux 7 (including Unbreakable Enterprise Kernel) - x86_64 FreeBSD 10 and 11 - AMD64 Fedora 24 and 25 - x86_64 SUSE 11 and 12 Enterprise - i586 SUSE 11 and 12 Enterprise - x86_64 Ubuntu 12.04, 12.10, 13.04, 13.10, 14.04, and 16.04 - i386 Ubuntu 12.04, 12.10, 13.04, 13.10, 14.04, and 16.04 - AMD64
Windows	Windows 7, 8, and 10 - i386 Windows Server 2008, Server 2008 R2, Server 2012, Server 2012 R2, Server 2016, 7, 8, and 10 - x86-64
macOS X	macOS X 10.8 - 10.13

- Browsers: Nessus supports the following browsers:
    - Google Chrome (50 and above)
    - Apple Safari (10 and above)
    - Mozilla Firefox (50 and above)
    - Internet Explorer (11 and above)
- PDF reports: The Nessus `.pdf` report generation feature requires the latest version of Oracle Java or OpenJDK. Install Oracle Java or OpenJDK prior to installing Nessus.

How to do it ...

Perform the following steps:

1. Download the applicable Nessus installation file from `https://www.tenable.com/downloads/nessus`, making sure to choose the correct file for the operating system in use.

For a 64-bit Windows operating system, download Nessus-7.1.3-x64.msi.

2. Register and obtain an activation code from `https://www.tenable.com/downloads/nessus`. A sample email with the Nessus activation code is shown in the following screenshot:

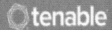

Nessus Home Evaluation

Welcome to Nessus Home and congratulations on taking action to secure your personal network! We offer the latest plugins for vulnerability scanning today, helping you identify more vulnerabilities and keep your personal network protected.

If you use Nessus in a professional capacity and want advanced capabilities such as unlimited assessments, or the ability to perform compliance checks or content audits, Nessus Professional may be better suited to your needs. To learn more view the Nessus Professional datasheet or request a free evaluation.

Activating Your Nessus Home Subscription

Your activation code for Nessus Home is:

▬▬▬▬▬▬▬▬▬▬

This is a one time code. If you uninstall and then reinstall you will need to register the scanner again and receive another activation code.

3. Install the downloaded `.msi` file by following the instructions.

4. Nessus requires you to create an admin user during the installation process, as follows:

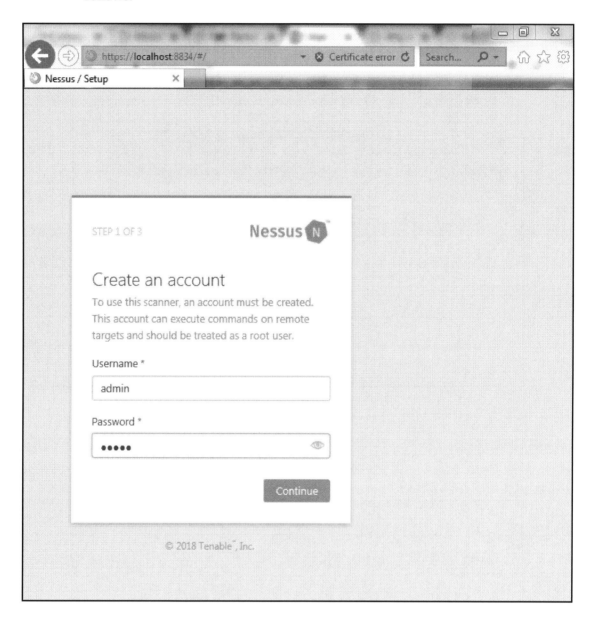

5. Insert the activation code received in the email from Tenable, as shown here:

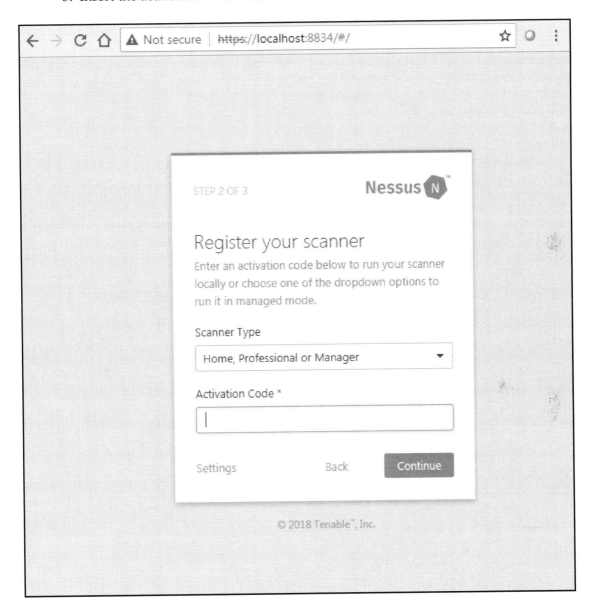

6. Ensure that the system is connected to the internet so that Nessus can auto-download plugins from its server.

How it works...

Once the user downloads and installs the executable file on the Windows operating system, the Nessus software can be accessed on a web interface on localhost at port 8834. In order for the installation to be completed, Nessus requires an activation code which can be obtained by registering on the Tenable website and providing some of your details. Once the key is obtained over email, you need to enter the activation code based on the usage and click **Continue** to be able to finish the installation by downloading plugins. Whenever a new vulnerability is identified, Tenable creates programs and scripts to identify these vulnerabilities. These scripts and programs are called plugins, written in **Nessus Attack Scripting Language** (**NASL**). These plugins are to be updated regularly to ensure that the Nessus scan has not left out any recently uncovered vulnerability. A typical plugin consists of vulnerability related information, such as a description, impact, remediation, and also some vulnerability metrics, such as CVSS and CVE.

With a machine connected to the internet, if you are using the Nessus browser interface for installation, the download of the plugins is an automatic process. You should see a plugin download screen once you have registered a license with Nessus. If installing Nessus offline, you will have to manually download the plugins from the custom-generated link once you have registered the license with Nessus. Download the plugins and extract the ZIP or TAR folder into the following directories, based on the operating system you are using:

- In Linux, install to the following directory:

    ```
    # /opt/nessus/sbin/
    ```

- In FreeBSD, install to the following directory:

    ```
    # /usr/local/nessus/sbin/
    ```

- In macOS X, install to the following directory:

  # /Library/Nessus/run/sbin/

- In Windows, install to the following directory: C:\Program
  Files\Tenable\Nessus

Once you extract the package, you can use the following commands to install these plugins based on the operating system in use:

- In Linux, use the following command:

  # /opt/nessus/sbin/nessuscli update <tar.gz filename>

- In FreeBSD, use the following command:

  # /usr/local/nessus/sbin/nessuscli update <tar.gz filename>

- In macOS X, use the following command:

  # /Library/Nessus/run/sbin/nessuscli update <tar.gz filename>

- In Windows, use the following command: C:\Program
  Files\Tenable\Nessus>nessuscli.exe update <tar.gz filename>

There's more...

If you have any issues in connecting to the internet, you can choose to activate offline, as shown in the following screenshot:

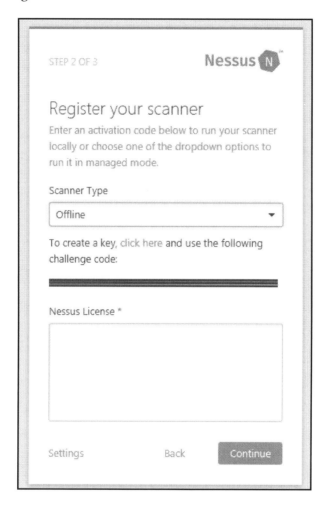

In order for the Nessus to be activated offline, a challenge code is displayed on your local browser where the Nessus instance is running, or can be displayed manually by using the following commands:

- On Linux, use the following command:

```
# /opt/nessus/sbin/nessuscli fetch --challenge
```

- On FreeBSD, use the following command:

  ```
  # /usr/local/nessus/sbin/nessuscli fetch --challenge
  ```

- On macOS X, use the following command:

  ```
  # /Library/Nessus/run/sbin/nessuscli fetch --challenge
  ```

- On Windows, use the following command:

  ```
  C:\Program Files\Tenable\Nessus>nessuscli.exe fetch --challenge
  ```

 The preceding commands are configured to the default installation directory. Change the directory to the location where Nessus is installed on your machine.

You can copy this challenge code onto a machine where the internet is available, and generate a license using the offline module on the Nessus website at https://plugins. nessus.org/v2/offline.php, and generate a license string. This license string can be used on the machine, in either the browser or offline mode, using the following commands:

- On Linux, use the following command:

  ```
  # /opt/nessus/sbin/nessuscli fetch --register-offline
  /opt/nessus/etc/nessus/nessus.license
  ```

- On FreeBSD, use the following command:

  ```
  # /usr/local/nessus/sbin/nessuscli fetch --register-offline
  /usr/local/nessus/etc/nessus/nessus.license
  ```

- On macOS X, use the following command:

  ```
  # /Library/Nessus/run/sbin/nessuscli fetch --register-offline
  /Library/Nessus/run/etc/nessus/nessus.license
  ```

- On Windows, use the following command:

  ```
  C:\Program Files\Tenable\Nessus>nessuscli.exe fetch --register-
  offline "C:\ProgramData\Tenable\Nessus\conf\nessus.license"
  ```

Downloading and installing Nmap

Nmap is a free and open source network scanning and audit tool available at `https://Nmap.org/`. This tool is one of the most important components of a network-level security audit, as it allows the user to monitor or observe the network-level posture of a host by providing data about open ports and services running on these ports. The Nmap tool also allows interaction with these services and the running of various scripts using Nmap Script Engine (NSE). The following command is the syntax to perform TCP syn full port scanning on the host `127.0.0.1`:

```
Nmap —sS —p1-65535 127.0.0.1
```

We will be looking into recipes for the usage of the Nmap tool in further chapters.

Getting ready

Nmap is available in various versions and formats based on the architecture and operating system supported by the user machine. Nmap also has a GUI version, called Zenmap, which provides better visibility of the options to select the commands to run. It is also available as a default tool as a part of operating systems used for exploitation and hacking techniques, such as Kali Linux. A user can choose the type or the version of Nmap based on their machine's configuration; for example, I am using a Windows 7 64-bit operating system, so I will choose the latest stable version of the executable that supports the 64-bit Windows 7 operating system. If you are using a 64-bit Linux or Unix distribution, there are rpm binary packages available for download at `https://Nmap.org/`.

How to do it...

Perform the following steps:

1. Download the applicable Nmap version from `http://www.Nmap.org/download.html`.
2. Right click on the downloaded file and select **Run as administrator**. This is required to ensure that the tool has all the privileges to be installed properly on your machine.

3. After this, you will be shown an open source license agreement. Read the agreement and click on **I agree**, as shown in the following screenshot:

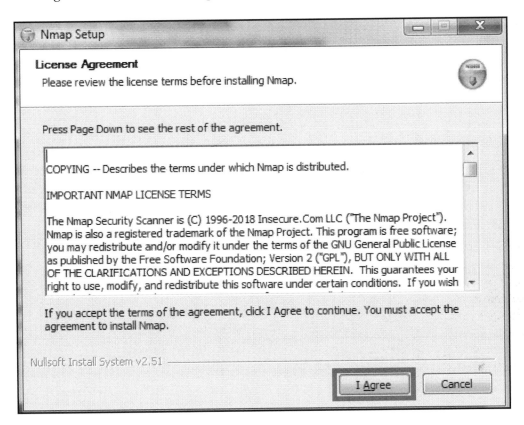

4. Choose various components to be installed as a part of the Nmap package. These utilities provide more functionality, such as packet generation and comparison. If you feel no need for these extra utilities, you can uncheck the feature, as in the following screenshot:

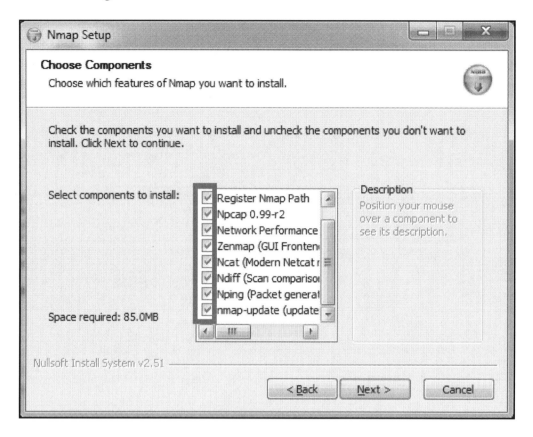

5. Select the location at which you want to install the tool. The tool suggests the C:\Program Files (x86)\Nmap\ path by default. Click **Next**.

6. The installation requires Npcap, the packet sniffing library of Windows for Nmap. Follow the instructions to install the Npcap to continue the installation of the Nmap and wait for the installation to finish.

How it works...

Once the installation is finished, open Command Prompt and type `Nmap`. If the Nmap tool is correctly installed, it should load the usage instructions of Nmap, shown as follows:

```
C:\Windows\system32\cmd.exe
Microsoft Windows [Version 6.1.7601]
Copyright (c) 2009 Microsoft Corporation.  All rights reserved.

C:\Users\admin>nmap
Nmap 7.70 ( https://nmap.org )
Usage: nmap [Scan Type(s)] [Options] {target specification}
TARGET SPECIFICATION:
  Can pass hostnames, IP addresses, networks, etc.
  Ex: scanme.nmap.org, microsoft.com/24, 192.168.0.1; 10.0.0-255.1-254
  -iL <inputfilename>: Input from list of hosts/networks
  -iR <num hosts>: Choose random targets
  --exclude <host1[,host2][,host3],...>: Exclude hosts/networks
  --excludefile <exclude_file>: Exclude list from file
HOST DISCOVERY:
  -sL: List Scan - simply list targets to scan
  -sn: Ping Scan - disable port scan
  -Pn: Treat all hosts as online -- skip host discovery
  -PS/PA/PU/PY[portlist]: TCP SYN/ACK, UDP or SCTP discovery to given ports
  -PE/PP/PM: ICMP echo, timestamp, and netmask request discovery probes
  -PO[protocol list]: IP Protocol Ping
  -n/-R: Never do DNS resolution/Always resolve [default: sometimes]
  --dns-servers <serv1[,serv2],...>: Specify custom DNS servers
  --system-dns: Use OS's DNS resolver
  --traceroute: Trace hop path to each host
```

There's more...

Installing Nmap on a Linux distribution is a different process. Most of the Linux-based operating systems have a single-step installation, using the package management utilities such as `yum` and `apt`.

Ensure that the machine is connected to the internet and execute the following commands:

- On CentOS, use the following command:

    ```
    yum install Nmap
    ```

- On Debian or Ubuntu, use the following command:

    ```
    apt-get install Nmap
    ```

Updating Nessus

Nessus can be updated either manually, or by scheduling automatic updates. The software update option can be found as a part of the **Settings** menu. This can be used to schedule daily, weekly, or monthly updates for Nessus software or even just the plugins. By default, Nessus uses its cloud server to download and install the updates, but you can also configure a custom server to download these updates.

Getting ready

You can update Nessus while connected to the internet or offline. If you want a hassle-free update or a quick one, you can ensure that the system is connected to the internet.

However, in order to update Nessus offline, you will have to download the update package from the Nessus website.

How to do it...

Follow these steps:

1. Navigate to **Settings**, then **Software Update** from the home page:

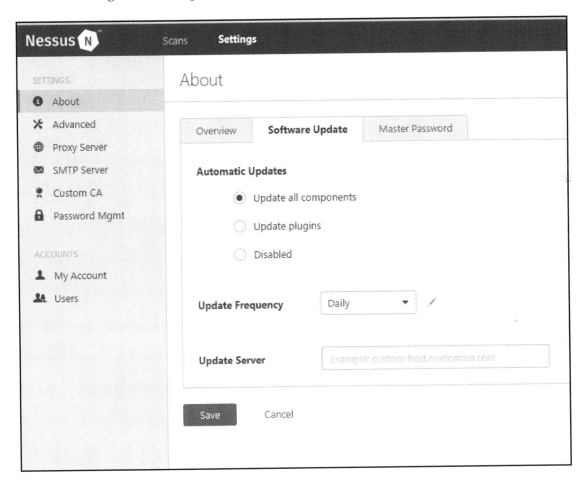

2. Choose the update frequency: **Daily**, **Weekly**, or **Monthly**.
3. Provide the server details if you have any internal or external servers from which you want Nessus to fetch updates.
4. Save the settings and they will be automatically applied.

5. In order to manually install the update, navigate to **Settings**, then **Software Update**, then **Manual Software Update**, as follows:

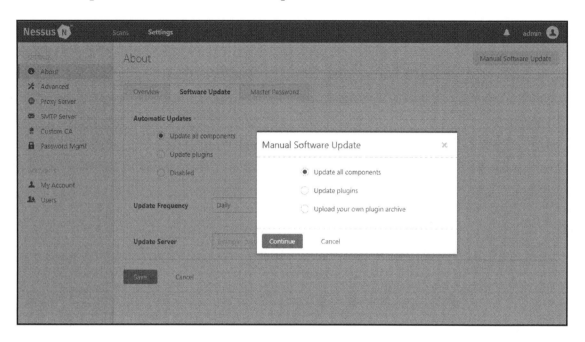

6. Select **Update all components** or **Update plugins** to instantly trigger an update.
7. If the machine is not connected to the internet, you can download the update package from the Tenable website and update it by selecting the option **Upload your own plugin archive**.

There's more...

Nessus has an evaluation license with a restriction on the number of IP addresses that you can scan, and a full license, bought for a certain length of time and without any restrictions on the number of IP addresses one can scan. A fully licensed version of Nessus is available at approximately $2,500 per scanner on the Nessus website:

1. Select the **Edit** option next to the **Activation Code**.
2. In the box displayed, select the type of Nessus in use.
3. In the **Activation Code** box, type your new activation code.
4. Select **Activate**.

Once done, Nessus downloads the plugins required and installs them automatically.

Updating Nmap

The most straightforward way to update Nmap is to download the latest available version of the software and manually install the package.

Getting ready

Download the latest stable version from `https://Nmap.org/download.html/`, making sure to choose the right version for the current operating system in use.

How to do it...

Perform the following steps:

1. Right-click on the downloaded file and select **Run as administrator**. This is required to ensure that the tool has all the privileges to be installed properly on your machine.
2. After this, you will be shown an open source license agreement. Read the agreement and click on **I agree**, as shown in the following screenshot:

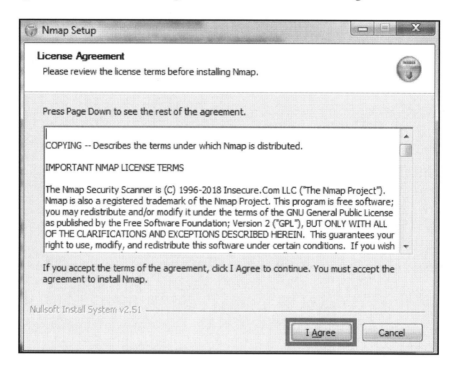

3. Choose which of the various components will be installed as a part of the Nmap package. These utilities provide additional functionality, such as packet generation and comparison. If you feel no need for these extra utilities, you can uncheck the features, as in the following screenshot:

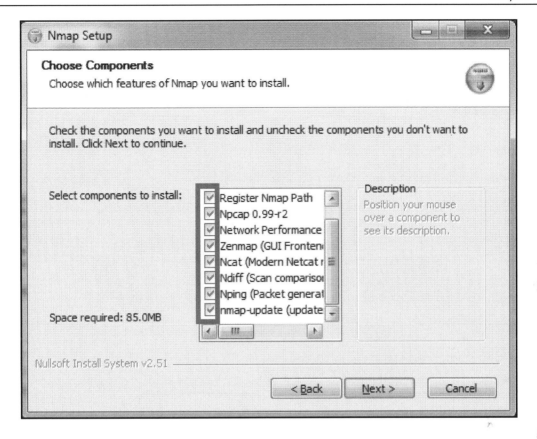

4. Select the location where you want to install the tool. `C:\Program Files (x86)\Nmap\` is the default path suggested by the tool. Then click **Next**.

5. The installation requires Npcap. This is the packet sniffing library of Windows for Nmap. Follow the instructions to install the Npcap and to continue the installation of the Nmap; wait for the installation to finish.

Removing Nessus

Removing the Nessus software is similar to removing Nmap. Once done, the port on which the service was running will be free and you will no longer be able to access the web interface.

Getting ready

The steps to remove Nessus vary from platform to platform. Before uninstalling Nessus, you may wish to back up all your policies and scan data by exporting them in the required format; for example, NessusDB.

How to do it...

Follow these steps to uninstall Nessus on Windows:

1. Navigate to the **Control Panel** on a Windows machine
2. Select **Uninstall or change a program**
3. Locate and select the Nessus package in the list of software installed
4. Click **Uninstall**

This will uninstall the Nessus software and its data from any Windows machine.

There's more...

Uninstalling Nessus on Linux is done as follows:

In order to determine the package name of Nessus, which is to be uninstalled, use the following commands for the different platforms:

- In Open Red Hat, CentOS, Oracle Linux, Fedora, SUSE, or FreeBSD, use the following command:

  ```
  # rpm -qa | grep Nessus
  ```

- In OpenDebian/Kali and Ubuntu, use the following command:

  ```
  # dpkg -l | grep Nessus
  ```

- In OpenFreeBSD, use the following command:

  ```
  # pkg_info | grep Nessus
  ```

Use the package info obtained from the preceding commands as the input to the following package removal commands for the respective platforms:

- In Open Red Hat, CentOS, Oracle Linux, Fedora, or SUSE, this looks as follows:

```
# rpm -e <Package Name>
```

- In Open Debian/Kali and Ubuntu, this looks as follows:

```
# dpkg -r <package name>
```

- In Open FreeBSD, this looks as follows:

```
# pkg delete <package name>
```

Remove the Nessus directory to delete any other files present using the commands mentioned here:

- In Open Linux, use the following command:

```
# rm -rf /opt/nessus
```

- In Open FreeBSD, use the following command:

```
# rm -rf /usr/local/Nessus
```

If you face any issues during the removal of Nessus, stop the Nessus daemon and try removing the files again.

Perform the following steps to uninstall Nessus on macOS:

1. Navigate to **System Preferences** and select **Nessus**
2. Select the **lock** option
3. Enter the username and password
4. Select the **Stop Nessus** button

Remove the following Nessus directories, subdirectories, or files:

- `/Library/Nessus`
- `/Library/LaunchDaemons/com.tenablesecurity.nessusd.plist`
- `/Library/PreferencePanes/Nessus Preferences.prefPane`
- `/Applications/Nessus`

Removal of these files will ensure that the software is completely uninstalled from the machine.

Removing Nmap

The uninstallation process of Nmap is pretty straightforward on both Windows and Linux. This will remove all the dependencies and libraries that have been installed by Nmap.

How to do it...

Follow these steps to uninstall Nmap on Windows:

1. Navigate to the **Control Panel** of the Windows machine
2. Select **Uninstall or change a program**
3. Locate and select the Nmap package in the list of software installed
4. Click **Uninstall**

This will uninstall the Nmap software and its data from any Windows machine.

There's more...

In Linux-based distributions you can simply delete all the folders pertaining to Nmap to uninstall Nmap from your machine. If you have installed Nmap from a downloaded source, there will exist an uninstallation script in the same folder that will uninstall Nmap from your machine. Furthermore, if it was installed in the default location, it can be removed using the following commands:

```
rm -f bin/Nmap bin/nmapfe bin/xnmap
rm -f man/man1/Nmap.1 man/man1/zenmap.1
rm -rf share/Nmap
./bin/uninstall_zenmap
```

3
Port Scanning

In this chapter, we will cover the following recipes:

- How to specify a target
- How to perform host discovery
- How to identify open ports
- How to manage specification and scan order
- How to perform script and version scan
- How to detect operating system
- How to detect and bypass network protection systems
- How to use Zenmap

Introduction

In this chapter, we will be going through various recipes that explain how to make use of Nmap to perform various port scanning techniques. Each recipe will contain practical insights into performing Nmap scans on a test virtual machine, allowing you to understand the functionalities of the various switches supported by Nmap.

How to specify a target

The nmap command interprets any content appended without an associated switch as a target. The following is a basic syntax that specifies an IP address or a hostname to scan without any associated switches:

```
nmap 127.0.0.1
nmap localhost
```

The hostname is resolved with the configured DNS server and the IP address is obtained to perform the scan. If multiple IP address are associated with one hostname, the first IP address will be scanned and the result will be displayed. The following syntax allows `nmap` to perform scans on all the IP addresses resolved with the hostname provided in the command:

nmap xyz.com*

Nmap also supports scanning the whole subnet, provided that you append the mask at the end of an IP address or hostname. Then, Nmap will consider all the resolved IP addresses in the range of the mask mentioned. For example, `10.0.0.1/24` would scan the `256` hosts between `10.0.0.1` and `10.0.0.255`, including `.1`, and `.255`. `10.0.0.21/24` would scan exactly the same targets.

Nmap also allows you to resolve an entire subnet and then exclude certain hosts from scanning. For example, the following syntax allows you to scan all the hosts resolved for `10.0.0.1/24` except any IP addresses whose last network bits are `.1` or `.255`:

nmap 10.0.0.2-254

This can be used in any of the four network bits, such as `10.0.1-254.1-254`, which will allow you to skip IP addresses `10.0.0.0`, `10.0.0.255`, `10.0.255.0`, and `10.0.255.255`. Nmap also supports fully qualified IPv6 addresses, but not octet range. For an IPv6 address with non-global scope, the zone suffix ID needs to be mentioned.

Nmap supports various input formats for a user to specify the targets. The following are the switches that can be used to mention the hosts on the specified format:

nmap -iL <inputfilename>

This will allow the user to create a text file with a list of all the IP addresses/range to be scanned. This is a feasible option when you have many IP addresses to be scanned. For example, if you want to scan all the IP addresses from different subnets for a medium-scale organization with more than 10,000 assets, it is not feasible to enter these IP addresses on the command line. Instead, create a text file with a list of all the IP addresses to be scanned and mention the filename with the absolute path after `-iL`. Nmap then fetches the list of IP addresses from the file and performs the scan:

```
nmap -iR <num hosts>
```

For large organizations and internet-based scans, you may want to scan random targets or identify unknown targets. The −iR switch with the appended number of random hosts to be identified for scans will allow the user to perform these operations. For example, if you are trying to identify eight random hosts with the ftp port open, the following syntax can be used:

```
nmap -sS -Pn -p 21 -iR 8 --open
```

The following syntax will help you to exclude servers when your input is a range of servers, a subnet, or a pre-existing large list of servers. The hosts mentioned along with this switch are omitted from scanning, thereby preventing the servers from being hit with any unwanted traffic:

```
nmap --exclude <host1>[,<host2>[,...]]
```

The following command works similarly to the preceding syntax, except that the host exclusion list is fetched from a file instead of manually mentioning the server list. This is feasible when the list of hosts to be excluded from the scan is long:

```
nmap --excludefile <exclude_file>
```

Getting ready

In order to perform this activity, you will have to satisfy the following prerequisites on your machine:

- Install Nmap.
- Provide network access to the hosts on which the scans are to be performed.

In order to install Nmap, you can follow the instructions provided in Chapter 2, *Understanding Network Scanning Tools*. This will allow you to download a compatible version of Nmap and install all the required plugins. In order to check whether your machine has Nmap installed, open Command Prompt and type Nmap.

If Nmap is installed, you will see a screen similar to the following screenshot:

```
C:\Windows\system32\cmd.exe
Microsoft Windows [Version 6.1.7601]
Copyright (c) 2009 Microsoft Corporation.  All rights reserved.

C:\Users\admin>nmap
Nmap 7.70 ( https://nmap.org )
Usage: nmap [Scan Type(s)] [Options] {target specification}
TARGET SPECIFICATION:
  Can pass hostnames, IP addresses, networks, etc.
  Ex: scanme.nmap.org, microsoft.com/24, 192.168.0.1; 10.0.0-255.1-254
  -iL <inputfilename>: Input from list of hosts/networks
  -iR <num hosts>: Choose random targets
  --exclude <host1[,host2][,host3],...>: Exclude hosts/networks
  --excludefile <exclude_file>: Exclude list from file
HOST DISCOVERY:
  -sL: List Scan - simply list targets to scan
  -sn: Ping Scan - disable port scan
  -Pn: Treat all hosts as online -- skip host discovery
  -PS/PA/PU/PY[portlist]: TCP SYN/ACK, UDP or SCTP discovery to given ports
  -PE/PP/PM: ICMP echo, timestamp, and netmask request discovery probes
  -PO[protocol list]: IP Protocol Ping
  -n/-R: Never do DNS resolution/Always resolve [default: sometimes]
  --dns-servers <serv1[,serv2],...>: Specify custom DNS servers
  --system-dns: Use OS's DNS resolver
  --traceroute: Trace hop path to each host
SCAN TECHNIQUES:
  -sS/sT/sA/sW/sM: TCP SYN/Connect<>/ACK/Window/Maimon scans
  -sU: UDP Scan
  -sN/sF/sX: TCP Null, FIN, and Xmas scans
  --scanflags <flags>: Customize TCP scan flags
```

If you do not see this screen, retry the step by moving the Command Prompt control into the folder where nmap is installed (C:\Program Files\nmap). If you do not see the screen even after doing this, remove and reinstall nmap.

To populate the open ports on hosts for which the scan is to be done, you are required to have network-level access to that particular host. A simple way to check whether you have access to the particular host is through ICMP by sending ping packets to the host. But this method works only if ICMP and ping is enabled in that network. If ICMP is disabled, live host detection technique varies, and we will see this in *How do it..* sections of this recipe.

The prerequisites for this recipe are common to all the other recipes in this chapter.

How do it...

Here are the steps:

1. Open nmap in Command Prompt.
2. Enter the following syntax in Command Prompt to scan the IP address 192.168.75.136:

   nmap 192.168.75.136

```
C:\Windows\system32\cmd.exe

Microsoft Windows [Version 6.1.7601]
Copyright (c) 2009 Microsoft Corporation.  All rights reserved.

C:\Users\admin>nmap 192.168.75.136
Starting Nmap 7.70 ( https://nmap.org ) at 2018-09-02 23:09 Arabian Standard Time
Nmap scan report for 192.168.75.136
Host is up (0.027s latency).
Not shown: 999 closed ports
PORT    STATE SERVICE
80/tcp open   http
MAC Address: 00:0C:29:5A:B2:9D (VMware)

Nmap done: 1 IP address (1 host up) scanned in 36.04 seconds
```

3. Enter the following syntax in Command Prompt to scan the IP addresses present in the ip.txt file:

   nmap -iL ip.txt

```
C:\Windows\system32\cmd.exe

C:\Users\admin>nmap -iL ip.txt
Starting Nmap 7.70 ( https://nmap.org ) at 2018-09-02 23:15 Arabian Standard Time
Nmap scan report for 192.168.75.136
Host is up (0.00038s latency).
Not shown: 999 closed ports
PORT    STATE SERVICE
80/tcp open   http
MAC Address: 00:0C:29:5A:B2:9D (VMware)

Nmap done: 1 IP address (1 host up) scanned in 34.04 seconds

C:\Users\admin>
```

4. Enter the following syntax in the Command Prompt to exclude the
   `192.168.75.136` IP address from the scan list:

```
nmap  -v 192.168.75.135/28 --exclude 192.168.75.136
```

```
C:\Windows\system32\cmd.exe

C:\Users\admin>nmap -v  192.168.75.135/28 --exclude 192.168.75.136
Starting Nmap 7.70 ( https://nmap.org ) at 2018-09-02 23:41 Arabian Standard Time
Initiating ARP Ping Scan at 23:41
Scanning 15 hosts [1 port/host]
Completed ARP Ping Scan at 23:41, 2.55s elapsed (15 total hosts)
Nmap scan report for 192.168.75.128 [host down]
Nmap scan report for 192.168.75.129 [host down]
Nmap scan report for 192.168.75.130 [host down]
Nmap scan report for 192.168.75.131 [host down]
Nmap scan report for 192.168.75.132 [host down]
Nmap scan report for 192.168.75.133 [host down]
Nmap scan report for 192.168.75.134 [host down]
Nmap scan report for 192.168.75.135 [host down]
Nmap scan report for 192.168.75.137 [host down]
Nmap scan report for 192.168.75.138 [host down]
Nmap scan report for 192.168.75.139 [host down]
Nmap scan report for 192.168.75.140 [host down]
Nmap scan report for 192.168.75.141 [host down]
Nmap scan report for 192.168.75.142 [host down]
Nmap scan report for 192.168.75.143 [host down]
Read data files from: C:\Program Files (x86)\Nmap
Nmap done: 15 IP addresses (0 hosts up) scanned in 16.17 seconds
         Raw packets sent: 30 (840B) | Rcvd: 0 (0B)

C:\Users\admin>
```

5. Enter the following syntax in the Command Prompt to exclude the IP addresses
   mentioned in the `ip.txt` file from the scan list:

```
nmap -v 192.168.75.135/28 --excludefile ip.txt
```

```
C:\Windows\system32\cmd.exe

C:\Users\admin>nmap -v 192.168.75.135/28 --excludefile ip.txt
Starting Nmap 7.70 ( https://nmap.org ) at 2018-09-02 23:44 Arabian Standard Time
Failed to resolve "ûv".
Stats: 0:00:09 elapsed; 0 hosts completed (0 up), 15 undergoing ARP Ping Scan
ARP Ping Scan Timing: About 3.33% done; ETC: 23:44 (0:00:29 remaining)
Nmap done: 15 IP addresses (0 hosts up) scanned in 23.52 seconds

C:\Users\admin>
```

How it works...

The options mentioned in this recipe help users to select targets at their convenience, irrespective of the size of their network or the provided list of hosts. Nmap does not require users to enter the final list of host to be scanned. Instead, as shown in this recipe, it provides various options to dynamically allow Nmap to select the targets based on various filters. The file-based filters allow Nmap to input a readily available list of hosts to be scanned, thereby reducing the effort required for customizations or formatting the lists.

How to perform host discovery

One of the basic techniques of identifying a running host is by sending an ICMP ping packet and analyzing the response to draw a conclusion. What if the host or the network is blocking ICMP packets at the network level or the host level? As per the ICMP technique, the host or the network will not pop up in the live host list. Host discovery is one of the core components of a network penetration test or vulnerability scan. A half-done host discovery can ignore hosts or networks from the scope and perform any further operation, thus leaving the network vulnerable.

Nmap provides various options and techniques to identify the live host by sending customized packets to satisfy specific network conditions. If no such options are provided, Nmap by default sends an ICMP echo to identify the live hosts. The provided probe options can be combined to increase the odds of identifying further ports. Once Nmap probes for the live hosts and obtains a list of live hosts, it scans for the open ports by default.

The following options are provided by Nmap to perform host discovery:

- −sL: This option lists the IP addresses present in the provided subnet. It also tries to resolve the IP addresses to their hostnames. The hostnames can help an attacker or a penetration tester find out a great deal about the network. You will not be able to combine this with any other options, such as OS discovery, because the functionality is to just list the IP addresses.
- −sn: This option tells Nmap not to perform a port scan once the host discovery is performed. Instead it just lists out the live IP addresses found. This uses an ICMP echo to identify the available hosts, which will not work if there is a firewall present in the network.

- -Pn (No ping): Generally, Nmap performs activities such as probing, port detection, service detection, and OS detection options only if the hosts are found live. This option allows Nmap to perform all the operations on the list of hosts provided to scan. For example, if a class C IP address with subnet /28 is specified, then Nmap performs probing on all the 255 hosts instead of checking for live hosts and performing the activity on them. This is an extensive scan option and generates a lot of traffic.

- -PS (port list): This option sends an empty TCP packet with SYN flag set. This is also called a syn ping packet. Generally, for a full TCP connection to happen, an ACK is generated by the host on receiving the SYN packet. Once the ACK packet is received, the Nmap host generates a SYN/ACK packet, which then establishes a connection. Instead, Nmap sends an RST, which is a reset flag packet, to drop the connection and thus declare the port to be open. This will allow you to determine the open ports without actually creating a connection, because any connection made will be logged at the network and system levels. This option also allows attackers to not leave any tracks while performing the detection.

 There is no space between -PS and the port number. You can specify a range of ports to perform the operation on as well.

- -PA(port list): This is similar to SYN scanning and is also known as the TCP ACK ping scan. Nmap generates TCP packets with ACK set. ACK basically acknowledges any data transferred over the connection, but there will be no existing connection from the Nmap machine to the host, thus it returns an RST-flag-enabled packet. This will allow Nmap to determine that the port is open and has a service functioning.

- -PU (port list): This is also similar to TCP scans, but this UDP ping scan is for UDP ports. For most ports the packet is empty, except for any service-specific ports, such as DNS and NTP. If a DNS ping packet reaches a closed port, the UDP probe should trigger an ICMP unreachable response from the host. If this response is not generated or the connection appears to be idle, it means that the port is functioning and a service is running on the port.

- -PY (port list): This switch generates an SCTP packet containing a part of INIT data. This means that you are trying to establish a connection. If the destination port is closed, an ABORT packet is sent back; otherwise, the connection moves on to the next step of a four-way handshake by replying with an INIT-ACK. Once the INIT-ACK is received, the Nmap machine sends an INIT-ACK and marks the port as open instead of creating a connection.

- -PO (protocol list): This protocol list scan allows Nmap to configure the packet with a couple of protocols enabled in the packet header, such as ICMP and IGMP, to see whether there are any host unreachable responses to determine that the protocols are not supported by the destination port, thereby marking the port as closed.

- -PR (ARP Ping): ARP scan allows Nmap to send ARP requests to the remote host. If there is any response then Nmap marks the host as live without examining any other results. This also supports IPv6.

- --disable-arp-ping: This allows a user to obtain specific results when a network device or proxy responds to the ARP requests, creating a situation where all the hosts appear to be up.

- --traceroute: Traceroute is a post scan module that determines the best port to use to reach the remote host. This works by sending low TTL packets.

- -n: This allows users to skip the DNS resolution process. This can be slow, and thus the scan takes a lot of time.

- -R: This option is the counterpart to -n. It mandates that Nmap performs reverse DNS resolutions for all the live hosts.

- --system-dns: This can be used to specify that the DNS servers used for resolution should be the DNS servers that are configured on the hosts.

- --dns-servers <server1>[,<server2>[,...]]: This option can be used to define specific DNS addresses to be used for reverse DNS resolution.

How do it...

These are the steps:

1. Open nmap in Command Prompt.

2. Run the following syntax in the Command Prompt to perform a live scan only, and not probe for a port scan:

   ```
   nmap -sn -v 192.168.75.135/28
   ```

```
C:\Windows\system32\cmd.exe

C:\Users\admin>nmap -sn -v 192.168.75.135/28
Starting Nmap 7.70 ( https://nmap.org ) at 2018-09-03 15:35 Arabian Standard Time
Initiating ARP Ping Scan at 15:35
Scanning 16 hosts [1 port/host]
Completed ARP Ping Scan at 15:35, 3.31s elapsed (16 total hosts)
Initiating Parallel DNS resolution of 16 hosts. at 15:35
Completed Parallel DNS resolution of 16 hosts. at 15:36, 16.50s elapsed
Nmap scan report for 192.168.75.128 [host down]
Nmap scan report for 192.168.75.129 [host down]
Nmap scan report for 192.168.75.130 [host down]
Nmap scan report for 192.168.75.131 [host down]
Nmap scan report for 192.168.75.132 [host down]
Nmap scan report for 192.168.75.133 [host down]
Nmap scan report for 192.168.75.134 [host down]
Nmap scan report for 192.168.75.135 [host down]
Nmap scan report for 192.168.75.136 [host down]
Nmap scan report for 192.168.75.137
Host is up (0.00s latency).
MAC Address: 00:0C:29:74:1C:63 (VMware)
Nmap scan report for 192.168.75.138 [host down]
Nmap scan report for 192.168.75.139 [host down]
Nmap scan report for 192.168.75.140 [host down]
Nmap scan report for 192.168.75.141 [host down]
Nmap scan report for 192.168.75.142 [host down]
Nmap scan report for 192.168.75.143 [host down]
Read data files from: C:\Program Files (x86)\Nmap
Nmap done: 16 IP addresses (1 host up) scanned in 34.25 seconds
           Raw packets sent: 31 (868B) | Rcvd: 1 (28B)

C:\Users\admin>
```

3. Run the following syntax in the Command Prompt to perform a no ping scan:

   ```
   nmap -Pn -v 192.168.75.135/28
   ```

```
C:\Windows\system32\cmd.exe

C:\Users\admin>nmap -Pn -v 192.168.75.135/28
Starting Nmap 7.70 ( https://nmap.org ) at 2018-09-03 15:39 Arabian Standard Time
Initiating ARP Ping Scan at 15:39
Scanning 16 hosts [1 port/host]
Completed ARP Ping Scan at 15:39, 2.84s elapsed (16 total hosts)
Initiating Parallel DNS resolution of 16 hosts. at 15:39
Completed Parallel DNS resolution of 16 hosts. at 15:40, 16.50s elapsed
Nmap scan report for 192.168.75.128 [host down]
Nmap scan report for 192.168.75.129 [host down]
Nmap scan report for 192.168.75.130 [host down]
Nmap scan report for 192.168.75.131 [host down]
Nmap scan report for 192.168.75.132 [host down]
Nmap scan report for 192.168.75.133 [host down]
Nmap scan report for 192.168.75.134 [host down]
Nmap scan report for 192.168.75.135 [host down]
Nmap scan report for 192.168.75.136 [host down]
Nmap scan report for 192.168.75.138 [host down]
Nmap scan report for 192.168.75.139 [host down]
Nmap scan report for 192.168.75.140 [host down]
Nmap scan report for 192.168.75.141 [host down]
Nmap scan report for 192.168.75.142 [host down]
Nmap scan report for 192.168.75.143 [host down]
Initiating SYN Stealth Scan at 15:40
Scanning 192.168.75.137 [1000 ports]
Discovered open port 25/tcp on 192.168.75.137
Discovered open port 3306/tcp on 192.168.75.137
Discovered open port 22/tcp on 192.168.75.137
Discovered open port 111/tcp on 192.168.75.137
Discovered open port 445/tcp on 192.168.75.137
Discovered open port 80/tcp on 192.168.75.137
Discovered open port 21/tcp on 192.168.75.137
Discovered open port 53/tcp on 192.168.75.137
Discovered open port 23/tcp on 192.168.75.137
Discovered open port 5900/tcp on 192.168.75.137
Discovered open port 139/tcp on 192.168.75.137
Discovered open port 1099/tcp on 192.168.75.137
Discovered open port 2121/tcp on 192.168.75.137
Discovered open port 6667/tcp on 192.168.75.137
Discovered open port 1524/tcp on 192.168.75.137
Discovered open port 8180/tcp on 192.168.75.137
Discovered open port 514/tcp on 192.168.75.137
Discovered open port 2049/tcp on 192.168.75.137
Discovered open port 513/tcp on 192.168.75.137
Discovered open port 6000/tcp on 192.168.75.137
Discovered open port 512/tcp on 192.168.75.137
Discovered open port 8009/tcp on 192.168.75.137
Discovered open port 5432/tcp on 192.168.75.137
Completed SYN Stealth Scan at 15:40, 0.10s elapsed (1000 total ports)
```

How it works...

These options help the user to streamline their requirement to identify the live hosts and thus perform further probes. Using these different scan options, a user can target a specific port and protocol to obtain the current status of the host. Most of these options can be further configured with advanced probing techniques, such as arguments for service detection and operating system detection, to obtain further information about these instances.

How to identify open ports

The following are the six port states that are present in Nmap:

- open: This means that the port is functioning and has a service running or accessing it. The service can thus accept any connections made as per the protocol and service in use on this port.

- closed: A closed port is not being accessed by any service, there is no service running on it. Thus, no connections made externally will be successful on these ports.

- filtered: This status is associated with ports from which no response was received due to the packet filtering mechanism present within the network. This might be caused by an intermediate network protection device.

- unfiltered: This status is associated with the ports that Nmap was not able to determine whether they were open or closed. Mostly ACK scan labels ports to be in unfiltered state; moreover, scans such as SYN and FIN can help resolve such issues.

- Open|filtered: Nmap classifies ports with this type when no response is received from them. The UDP, IP protocol, FIN, NULL, and Xmas scans associate this status with the ports.

- closed|filtered: This status is associated with ports that Nmap was not able to determine whether they were open or closed. Only idle scans use this status. Nmap provides various scan options for the user to craft a packet to obtain the desired result for Nmap to classify whether the port is open or closed. Most of these scan types are only allowed for administrative users because they have access to creating and sending raw packets.

- -sS (TCP SYN Scan): This is also called a half-open scan because TCP requires a three-way handshake to be completed before a connection is established. The Nmap machine generates a TCP SYN packet to which the remote port responds with TCP ACK, and then instead of sending a SYN/ACK packet, Nmap sends an RST flag to destroy the handshake, thereby preventing a connection. The port is considered if the Nmap SYN packet receives an ACK or SYN packet as a response.

- -sT (TCP connect scan): If a user does not have the required privileges to send a raw packet, or when a SYN scan is not an option, a TCP connect scan is used. As the name suggests, Nmap performs a complete three-way handshake and creates a connection to consider a port to be open.

- `-sU` (`UDP scans`): UDP scans send a packet to well-known ports, such as `53` and `61`, and it can then be performed on all ports. It sends protocol-specific packets to the famous ports and a generic UDP packet to the remaining ports. If the ports scanned return an ICMP unreachable error, then the port is closed. But if there is no response from a port it is marked as open filtered. In order to find out whether the port is actually running a service and is open, we can run a service detection scan.

- `-sY` (`SCTP INIT scan`): The SCTP INIT scan has already been discussed in the *How to perform host discovery* section. In order to perform this scan, there should be a running SCTP module.

- `-sN`; `-sF`; `-sX` (`TCP NULL, FIN, and Xmas scans`): In order to perform a deeper probe, Nmap provides an option to craft packets with different flags, such as FIN, PSH, and URG. If no flags are set, then it is called a Null scan. If FIN flags are set, then it is called a FIN scan, and if all three flags are set, then it is called an Xmas scan.

- `-sA` (`TCP ACK scan`): The TCP ACK scan has already been discussed in the *How to perform host discovery* section.

- `-sW` (`TCP Window scan`): The TCP Window scan works by the value of the TCP Window field of the RST packets received. Most systems have a window of zero for the RST packet of closed ports and a positive value for the open ports. This lists the port as closed instead of unfiltered once the RST packet is received.

- `--scanflags` (`Custom TCP scan`): The `Custom TCP scan` allows a user to set various flags in the TCP packet, such as URG, SYN, ACK, FIN, PSH, URG, and RST, thereby allowing the user to create a custom packet for the probe.

- `-sO` (`IP protocol scan`): This scan allows you to define the protocol for which the scan is being performed, such as TCP, UDP, ICMP, and IGMP, thus a specific packet is created for the probe.

- `-b <FTP relay host>` (`FTP bounce scan`): This allows the user to connect to one FTP host and then relay the files to another FTP host, which is mentioned in the argument.

How do it...

These are the steps:

1. Open nmap in Command Prompt.
2. Run the following syntax in the Command Prompt to perform a TCP SYN scan:

```
nmap -v -sS 192.168.75.137
```

```
C:\Windows\system32\cmd.exe

C:\Users\admin>nmap -v -sS 192.168.75.137
Starting Nmap 7.70 ( https://nmap.org ) at 2018-09-03 23:16 Arabian Standard Time
Initiating ARP Ping Scan at 23:16
Scanning 192.168.75.137 [1 port]
Completed ARP Ping Scan at 23:16, 1.38s elapsed (1 total hosts)
Initiating Parallel DNS resolution of 1 host. at 23:16
Completed Parallel DNS resolution of 1 host. at 23:16, 16.51s elapsed
Initiating SYN Stealth Scan at 23:16
Scanning 192.168.75.137 [1000 ports]
Discovered open port 80/tcp on 192.168.75.137
Discovered open port 3306/tcp on 192.168.75.137
Discovered open port 22/tcp on 192.168.75.137
Discovered open port 445/tcp on 192.168.75.137
Discovered open port 111/tcp on 192.168.75.137
Discovered open port 5900/tcp on 192.168.75.137
Discovered open port 2121/tcp on 192.168.75.137
Discovered open port 513/tcp on 192.168.75.137
Discovered open port 512/tcp on 192.168.75.137
Discovered open port 6000/tcp on 192.168.75.137
Discovered open port 5432/tcp on 192.168.75.137
Discovered open port 514/tcp on 192.168.75.137
Discovered open port 2049/tcp on 192.168.75.137
Discovered open port 1099/tcp on 192.168.75.137
Discovered open port 6667/tcp on 192.168.75.137
Discovered open port 8009/tcp on 192.168.75.137
Discovered open port 8180/tcp on 192.168.75.137
Discovered open port 1524/tcp on 192.168.75.137
Discovered open port 21/tcp on 192.168.75.137
Discovered open port 23/tcp on 192.168.75.137
Discovered open port 53/tcp on 192.168.75.137
Discovered open port 25/tcp on 192.168.75.137
Discovered open port 139/tcp on 192.168.75.137
Completed SYN Stealth Scan at 23:17, 1.11s elapsed (1000 total ports)
Nmap scan report for 192.168.75.137
Host is up (0.0023s latency).
Not shown: 977 closed ports
PORT      STATE SERVICE
21/tcp    open  ftp
22/tcp    open  ssh
23/tcp    open  telnet
25/tcp    open  smtp
53/tcp    open  domain
80/tcp    open  http
111/tcp   open  rpcbind
139/tcp   open  netbios-ssn
445/tcp   open  microsoft-ds
512/tcp   open  exec
513/tcp   open  login
514/tcp   open  shell
1099/tcp  open  rmiregistry
1524/tcp  open  ingreslock
2049/tcp  open  nfs
2121/tcp  open  ccproxy-ftp
3306/tcp  open  mysql
5432/tcp  open  postgresql
5900/tcp  open  vnc
```

3. Run the following syntax in the Command Prompt to perform a TCP Connect scan:

```
nmap -v -sT 192.168.75.137
```

```
C:\Windows\system32\cmd.exe - nmap -v -sT 192.168.75.137

C:\Users\admin>nmap -v -sT 192.168.75.137
Starting Nmap 7.70 ( https://nmap.org ) at 2018-09-03 23:18 Arabian Standard Time
Initiating ARP Ping Scan at 23:18
Scanning 192.168.75.137 [1 port]
Completed ARP Ping Scan at 23:18, 1.43s elapsed (1 total hosts)
Initiating Parallel DNS resolution of 1 host. at 23:18
Completed Parallel DNS resolution of 1 host. at 23:18, 16.50s elapsed
Initiating Connect Scan at 23:18
Scanning 192.168.75.137 [1000 ports]
Discovered open port 111/tcp on 192.168.75.137
Discovered open port 53/tcp on 192.168.75.137
Discovered open port 80/tcp on 192.168.75.137
Discovered open port 3306/tcp on 192.168.75.137
Discovered open port 445/tcp on 192.168.75.137
Discovered open port 21/tcp on 192.168.75.137
Discovered open port 139/tcp on 192.168.75.137
Discovered open port 23/tcp on 192.168.75.137
Discovered open port 5900/tcp on 192.168.75.137
Discovered open port 22/tcp on 192.168.75.137
Discovered open port 25/tcp on 192.168.75.137
Discovered open port 512/tcp on 192.168.75.137
Discovered open port 6000/tcp on 192.168.75.137
Discovered open port 2049/tcp on 192.168.75.137
Connect Scan Timing: About 15.10% done; ETC: 23:22 (0:02:54 remaining)
Discovered open port 5432/tcp on 192.168.75.137
Connect Scan Timing: About 29.47% done; ETC: 23:22 (0:02:26 remaining)
Discovered open port 8180/tcp on 192.168.75.137
Connect Scan Timing: About 44.40% done; ETC: 23:22 (0:01:54 remaining)
Connect Scan Timing: About 57.73% done; ETC: 23:22 (0:01:29 remaining)
Discovered open port 2121/tcp on 192.168.75.137
Discovered open port 513/tcp on 192.168.75.137
Connect Scan Timing: About 70.37% done; ETC: 23:22 (0:01:04 remaining)
Discovered open port 514/tcp on 192.168.75.137
Discovered open port 1524/tcp on 192.168.75.137
Discovered open port 8009/tcp on 192.168.75.137
Discovered open port 1099/tcp on 192.168.75.137
Connect Scan Timing: About 84.87% done; ETC: 23:22 (0:00:32 remaining)
Discovered open port 6667/tcp on 192.168.75.137
```

4. Run the following syntax in the Command Prompt to perform a TCP NULL scan:

```
nmap -v -sN 192.168.75.137
```

```
C:\Windows\system32\cmd.exe

C:\Users\admin>nmap -v -sN 192.168.75.137
Starting Nmap 7.70 ( https://nmap.org ) at 2018-09-03 23:22 Arabian Standard Time
Initiating ARP Ping Scan at 23:23
Scanning 192.168.75.137 [1 port]
Completed ARP Ping Scan at 23:23, 1.45s elapsed (1 total hosts)
Initiating Parallel DNS resolution of 1 host. at 23:23
Completed Parallel DNS resolution of 1 host. at 23:23, 16.50s elapsed
Initiating NULL Scan at 23:23
Scanning 192.168.75.137 [1000 ports]
Completed NULL Scan at 23:23, 1.21s elapsed (1000 total ports)
Nmap scan report for 192.168.75.137
Host is up (0.0033s latency).
Not shown: 977 closed ports
PORT      STATE         SERVICE
21/tcp    open|filtered ftp
22/tcp    open|filtered ssh
23/tcp    open|filtered telnet
25/tcp    open|filtered smtp
53/tcp    open|filtered domain
80/tcp    open|filtered http
111/tcp   open|filtered rpcbind
139/tcp   open|filtered netbios-ssn
445/tcp   open|filtered microsoft-ds
512/tcp   open|filtered exec
513/tcp   open|filtered login
514/tcp   open|filtered shell
1099/tcp  open|filtered rmiregistry
1524/tcp  open|filtered ingreslock
2049/tcp  open|filtered nfs
2121/tcp  open|filtered ccproxy-ftp
3306/tcp  open|filtered mysql
5432/tcp  open|filtered postgresql
5900/tcp  open|filtered vnc
6000/tcp  open|filtered X11
6667/tcp  open|filtered irc
8009/tcp  open|filtered ajp13
8180/tcp  open|filtered unknown
MAC Address: 00:0C:29:74:1C:63 (VMware)

Read data files from: C:\Program Files (x86)\Nmap
Nmap done: 1 IP address (1 host up) scanned in 28.52 seconds
           Raw packets sent: 1024 (40.948KB) | Rcvd: 978 (39.108KB)
```

How it works...

These options help the user to streamline their requirement to identify the open ports and thus perform further attacks. Using these different port scan options, a user can target a specific port and protocol to obtain the current status of the port. Further reconnaissance can be performed on the port by obtaining the exact service name and the version, which we will see in further sections of the book.

How to manage specification and scan order

Nmap provides various options to specify ports to be scanned in a random or sequential order. All the Nmap scans, without any ports specified or any specific NSE script provided as an argument, by default scan only the top 1,000 ports:

- `-p <port ranges>`: This option can be used to configure the ports to be scanned in multiple formats. It can be a range or a list. General representation of the syntax would be `-p1-65535` if you want to perform a full port scan or `-p1, 2, 3,` or `4` as a random list that can be non-serial in nature.

- `--exclude-ports <port ranges>`: It is a tedious task to prepare a list of ports to be scanned when the requirement is a full port with a few exclusions. In such cases, you can use the exclude ports flag to exclude the ports that are not to be scanned.

- `-F (Fast (limited port) scan)`: The fast scan further reduces the default number of ports scanned from 1,000 to 100. This will reduce the scan time immensely and thus provide quicker results, as the name suggests.

- `-r (Don't randomize ports)`: By default, Nmap randomizes the port order for the scan. This option allows the user to instruct Nmap to follow a strict order for the ports to be scanned.

- `--port-ratio <ratio>`: This scans all ports in the Nmap-services file with a ratio greater than the one given. `<ratio>` must be between `0.0` and `1.0`.

- `--top-ports <n>`: This scans the `<n>` highest-ratio ports found in the Nmap-services file after excluding all ports specified by `--exclude-ports`. `<n>` must be `1` or greater.

How do it...

Here are the steps:

1. Open nmap in Command Prompt.

2. Run the following syntax in the Command Prompt to perform a scan between ports 0-100:

   nmap 192.168.75.137 -p0-100

```
C:\Windows\system32\cmd.exe

C:\Users\admin>nmap 192.168.75.137 -p0-100
Starting Nmap 7.70 ( https://nmap.org ) at 2018-09-03 23:43 Arabian Standard Time
Nmap scan report for 192.168.75.137
Host is up (0.0028s latency).
Not shown: 95 closed ports
PORT   STATE SERVICE
21/tcp open  ftp
22/tcp open  ssh
23/tcp open  telnet
25/tcp open  smtp
53/tcp open  domain
80/tcp open  http
MAC Address: 00:0C:29:74:1C:63 (VMware)

Nmap done: 1 IP address (1 host up) scanned in 27.87 seconds

C:\Users\admin>
```

3. Run the following syntax in the Command Prompt to perform a fast scan on the top 100 ports:

   nmap -F 192.168.75.137

4. Run the following syntax in the Command Prompt to perform a scan without any port specification:

```
nmap 192.168.75.137
```

How it works...

Providing options to specify the ports in both ranges and lists will allow the user to optimize their scans, thereby delivering quicker results, as a full port scan in general takes 10 times longer than a 1,000-port scan or a port-specified scan. This will also allow the user to find out hosts with specific ports open.

How to perform a script and version scan

While performing penetration tests, reconnaissance is really important for informing the next steps of testing. Even though Nmap provides the open ports and the version of the service running on the port, you will need to know the exact version or the name of the service that is running to prepare further exploits or to gain further knowledge of the system.

The Nmap-service-probes database contains specific packet construction techniques to probe specific services and analyze the responses received from them. Nmap provides information about the service protocol, the application name, the version number, the hostname, the device type, and the OS family. It also sometimes determines whether the service is open to connections or if any default logins are available for the service:

- `-sV` (version detection): This flag enables Nmap to perform version detection on the particular host. This flag has options that can be used in conjunction with it.
- `--allports`: Nmap skips some ports that have a default function enabled when a connection is made. This option will enable users to skip any such exclusions and perform an all-port scan as per the syntax provided.
- `--version-intensity <intensity>`: This defines the intensity with which the probes are configured to determine the version. The value of this flag has a range between `0-9`, the default being `7`. The higher the value, the better the chances of the service versions being accurate.

- `--version-light`: This is used to configure lighter probes to reduce the scan time.
- `--version-all`: This sets the probe intensity at 9, thereby making the scan slower and the results having a chance of being more accurate.
- `--version-trace`: This prints out a lot of information about the version scans that are being performed.

How do it...

Here are the steps:

1. Open nmap in Command Prompt.
2. Run the following syntax in the Command Prompt to perform a service scan on the port range 0-100:

```
nmap -sV 192.168.75.137 -p0-100
```

```
C:\Users\admin>nmap -sV 192.168.75.137 -p0-100
Starting Nmap 7.70 ( https://nmap.org ) at 2018-09-04 00:14 Arabian Standard Time
Nmap scan report for 192.168.75.137
Host is up (0.0029s latency).
Not shown: 95 closed ports
PORT   STATE SERVICE VERSION
21/tcp open  ftp     vsftpd 2.3.4
22/tcp open  ssh     OpenSSH 4.7p1 Debian 8ubuntu1 (protocol 2.0)
23/tcp open  telnet  Linux telnetd
25/tcp open  smtp    Postfix smtpd
53/tcp open  domain  ISC BIND 9.4.2
80/tcp open  http    Apache httpd 2.2.8 ((Ubuntu) DAV/2)
MAC Address: 00:0C:29:74:1C:63 (VMware)
Service Info: Host: metasploitable.localdomain; OSs: Unix, Linux; CPE: cpe:/o:linux:linux_kernel

Service detection performed. Please report any incorrect results at https://nmap.org/submit/ .
Nmap done: 1 IP address (1 host up) scanned in 42.49 seconds

C:\Users\admin>
```

3. Run the following syntax in the Command Prompt to perform a service scan on the port range `0-100` and see debug info of the scan:

```
nmap -sV 192.168.75.137 -p0-100 --version-trace
```

How it works ...

A version scan helps the user obtain approximate version and name of the service running. For example, if a user identifies that a certain version of the FTP is running on the remote host, they can search for related exploits for that version as there will be version-dependent vulnerabilities.

How to detect operating system

Nmap uses TCP/IP stack fingerprinting for OS detection. This is done by crafting custom TCP and UDP packets and analyzing their responses. After generating various such probes and comparing the results to the Nmap-os-db database of more than 2,600 known OS fingerprints and provides the OS version. The fingerprint provides details such as the vendor name, OS name, OS generation, device type, and also their Common Platform Enumeration (CPE) representation. Nmap also provides an option for the user to submit the fingerprint obtained if it is not present in the Nmap database of operating signatures:

- -O (Enable OS detection): This enables OS detection for an Nmap scan. This flag further has options that can be used in conjunction with it.
- --osscan-limit: This option will reduce the scan time when a list of hosts is being scanned by skipping the hosts with no ports open for OS detection, thereby providing faster results for live hosts.
- --osscan-guess; --fuzzy: If Nmap is not able to identify the OS, it tries to provide the closest signature, and the similarities between the signatures should be very high. The flags listed here will allow Nmap to guess more aggressively whether the exact OS has been found.
- --max-os-tries: Nmap by default retries five times if the operating system probe is not able to identify a perfect match. This will allow the users to limit these tries and thus save a lot of scan time.

How do it...

Here are the steps:

1. Open nmap in Command Prompt.
2. Run the following syntax in the Command Prompt to perform OS detection:

   ```
   nmap -O 192.168.75.137
   ```

```
C:\Windows\system32\cmd.exe

C:\Users\admin>nmap -O 192.168.75.137
Starting Nmap 7.70 ( https://nmap.org ) at 2018-09-04 00:41 Arabian Standard Time
Nmap scan report for 192.168.75.137
Host is up (0.00069s latency).
Not shown: 977 closed ports
PORT      STATE SERVICE
21/tcp    open  ftp
22/tcp    open  ssh
23/tcp    open  telnet
25/tcp    open  smtp
53/tcp    open  domain
80/tcp    open  http
111/tcp   open  rpcbind
139/tcp   open  netbios-ssn
445/tcp   open  microsoft-ds
512/tcp   open  exec
513/tcp   open  login
514/tcp   open  shell
1099/tcp  open  rmiregistry
1524/tcp  open  ingreslock
2049/tcp  open  nfs
2121/tcp  open  ccproxy-ftp
3306/tcp  open  mysql
5432/tcp  open  postgresql
5900/tcp  open  vnc
6000/tcp  open  X11
6667/tcp  open  irc
8009/tcp  open  ajp13
8180/tcp  open  unknown
MAC Address: 00:0C:29:74:1C:63 (VMware)
Device type: general purpose
Running: Linux 2.6.X
OS CPE: cpe:/o:linux:linux_kernel:2.6
OS details: Linux 2.6.9 - 2.6.33
Network Distance: 1 hop

OS detection performed. Please report any incorrect results at https://nmap.org/submit/ .
Nmap done: 1 IP address (1 host up) scanned in 29.78 seconds

C:\Users\admin>
```

How it works...

Identifying the operating system running on a remote host could be of great use to any vulnerability scanning or penetration testing process, as this will allow you to differentiate between the applicable vulnerabilities and exploits.

How to detect and bypass network protection systems

The basic function of Nmap is to generate custom packets and analyze their response once they are sent to the remote hosts. This sometimes is not allowed by network protection systems such as firewalls and intrusion prevention and detection systems. In this recipe, we will discuss some of the methods that can be used to bypass these protections:

- `-f` (Fragment packets): Most firewalls perform stateful and stateless packet inspection for which they examine the content of the packets and decide whether to allow the packet or drop it based on its contents. In order to bypass this, Nmap provides an option to fragment the packets so that the network device will not be able to construct the packet to read the correct contents, thereby bypassing the protection.

- `--mtu` (Maximum transmission unit specification): This works similar to the preceding method of creating packets of different sizes. With MTU you can specify the packet size in multiples of 8, such as 8, 16, 24, 32, and so on. This will allow Nmap to create packets of this size, thereby bypassing the protection.

- `-D` (decoy address): This will allow Nmap to generate packets from a decoy address. This will generate similar traffic with multiple source IP addresses, thereby making it difficult for the network protection system to determine the source of traffic generation.

- `--source-port` (Source port specification): If the network device is configured to disallow traffic generated by Nmap from a specific port, setting a random port number using this option will allow you to bypass this configuration on the network protection system.

- `--data-length` (Random data append): Using this option, you can add data to the packet generated by Nmap and then create a packet with a lot of unnecessary random data, making it difficult for the network protection system to understand and block the traffic.

- `--randomize-hosts` (Randomizing hosts): This option will allow Nmap to scan the hosts randomly by generating pattern-less traffic, which could be ignored by the network protection system.

- `--spoof-mac` (MAC address spoofing): This option will allow the user to bypass any MAC address restriction put in place by the network protection systems.

How do it...

Here are the steps:

1. Open nmap in the Command Prompt.

2. Run the following syntax in the Command Prompt to perform a scan to generate fragmented packets:

   ```
   nmap -f 192.168.75.137
   ```

```
C:\Windows\system32\cmd.exe

C:\Users\admin>nmap -f 192.168.75.137
Warning: Packet fragmentation selected on a host other than Linux, OpenBSD, FreeBSD, or NetBSD.
Starting Nmap 7.70 ( https://nmap.org ) at 2018-09-04 01:09 Arabian Standard Time
Nmap scan report for 192.168.75.137
Host is up (0.0025s latency).
Not shown: 977 closed ports
PORT      STATE SERVICE
21/tcp    open  ftp
22/tcp    open  ssh
23/tcp    open  telnet
25/tcp    open  smtp
53/tcp    open  domain
80/tcp    open  http
111/tcp   open  rpcbind
139/tcp   open  netbios-ssn
445/tcp   open  microsoft-ds
512/tcp   open  exec
513/tcp   open  login
514/tcp   open  shell
1099/tcp  open  rmiregistry
1524/tcp  open  ingreslock
2049/tcp  open  nfs
2121/tcp  open  ccproxy-ftp
3306/tcp  open  mysql
5432/tcp  open  postgresql
5900/tcp  open  vnc
6000/tcp  open  X11
6667/tcp  open  irc
8009/tcp  open  ajp13
8180/tcp  open  unknown
MAC Address: 00:0C:29:74:1C:63 (VMware)

Nmap done: 1 IP address (1 host up) scanned in 27.30 seconds

C:\Users\admin>
```

3. Run the following syntax in the Command Prompt to perform a scan to generate packets with the MTU specification:

   ```
   nmap -mtu 24 192.168.75.137
   ```

```
C:\Windows\system32\cmd.exe

C:\Users\admin>nmap --mtu 24 192.168.75.137
Warning: Packet fragmentation selected on a host other than Linux, OpenBSD, FreeBSD, or NetBSD.
Starting Nmap 7.70 ( https://nmap.org ) at 2018-09-04 01:11 Arabian Standard Time
Nmap scan report for 192.168.75.137
Host is up (0.0026s latency).
Not shown: 977 closed ports
PORT      STATE SERVICE
21/tcp    open  ftp
22/tcp    open  ssh
23/tcp    open  telnet
25/tcp    open  smtp
53/tcp    open  domain
80/tcp    open  http
111/tcp   open  rpcbind
139/tcp   open  netbios-ssn
445/tcp   open  microsoft-ds
512/tcp   open  exec
513/tcp   open  login
514/tcp   open  shell
1099/tcp open  rmiregistry
1524/tcp open  ingreslock
2049/tcp open  nfs
2121/tcp open  ccproxy-ftp
3306/tcp open  mysql
5432/tcp open  postgresql
5900/tcp open  vnc
6000/tcp open  X11
6667/tcp open  irc
8009/tcp open  ajp13
8180/tcp open  unknown
MAC Address: 00:0C:29:74:1C:63 (VMware)

Nmap done: 1 IP address (1 host up) scanned in 27.57 seconds

C:\Users\admin>
```

4. Run the following syntax in the Command Prompt to perform a decoy scan from the IP address mentioned:

```
nmap -D 192.168.75.138 192.168.75.137
```

```
C:\Windows\system32\cmd.exe

C:\Users\admin>nmap -D 192.168.75.138 192.168.75.137
Starting Nmap 7.70 ( https://nmap.org ) at 2018-09-04 01:18 Arabian Standard Time
Nmap scan report for 192.168.75.137
Host is up (0.0015s latency).
Not shown: 977 closed ports
PORT      STATE SERVICE
21/tcp    open  ftp
22/tcp    open  ssh
23/tcp    open  telnet
25/tcp    open  smtp
53/tcp    open  domain
80/tcp    open  http
111/tcp   open  rpcbind
139/tcp   open  netbios-ssn
445/tcp   open  microsoft-ds
512/tcp   open  exec
513/tcp   open  login
514/tcp   open  shell
1099/tcp open  rmiregistry
1524/tcp open  ingreslock
2049/tcp open  nfs
2121/tcp open  ccproxy-ftp
3306/tcp open  mysql
5432/tcp open  postgresql
5900/tcp open  vnc
6000/tcp open  X11
6667/tcp open  irc
8009/tcp open  ajp13
8180/tcp open  unknown
MAC Address: 00:0C:29:74:1C:63 (VMware)

Nmap done: 1 IP address (1 host up) scanned in 30.50 seconds
```

5. Run the following syntax in the Command Prompt to perform a scan to append random data to the packets:

```
nmap -v  --data-length 25 192.168.75.137
```

```
C:\Windows\system32\cmd.exe

C:\Users\admin>nmap -v --data-length 25 192.168.75.137
Starting Nmap 7.70 ( https://nmap.org ) at 2018-09-04 01:24 Arabian Standard Time
Initiating ARP Ping Scan at 01:24
Scanning 192.168.75.137 [1 port]
Completed ARP Ping Scan at 01:24, 1.56s elapsed (1 total hosts)
Initiating Parallel DNS resolution of 1 host. at 01:24
Completed Parallel DNS resolution of 1 host. at 01:24, 16.50s elapsed
Initiating SYN Stealth Scan at 01:24
Scanning 192.168.75.137 [1000 ports]
Discovered open port 445/tcp on 192.168.75.137
Discovered open port 5900/tcp on 192.168.75.137
Discovered open port 80/tcp on 192.168.75.137
Discovered open port 139/tcp on 192.168.75.137
Discovered open port 53/tcp on 192.168.75.137
Discovered open port 3306/tcp on 192.168.75.137
Discovered open port 25/tcp on 192.168.75.137
Discovered open port 111/tcp on 192.168.75.137
Discovered open port 23/tcp on 192.168.75.137
Discovered open port 22/tcp on 192.168.75.137
Discovered open port 21/tcp on 192.168.75.137
Discovered open port 1099/tcp on 192.168.75.137
Discovered open port 8180/tcp on 192.168.75.137
Discovered open port 1524/tcp on 192.168.75.137
Discovered open port 512/tcp on 192.168.75.137
Discovered open port 6667/tcp on 192.168.75.137
Discovered open port 8009/tcp on 192.168.75.137
Discovered open port 5432/tcp on 192.168.75.137
Discovered open port 6000/tcp on 192.168.75.137
Discovered open port 2121/tcp on 192.168.75.137
Discovered open port 514/tcp on 192.168.75.137
Discovered open port 2049/tcp on 192.168.75.137
Discovered open port 513/tcp on 192.168.75.137
Completed SYN Stealth Scan at 01:24, 0.07s elapsed (1000 total ports)
```

How it works...

Network protection systems such as firewalls and intrusion prevention and detection systems can result in false positives by dropping packets that consist of probes generated by Nmap. The bypass techniques can be used to develop better results in reconnaissance.

How to use Zenmap

Zenmap is the graphical interface of Nmap. It is open source and comes in the same installation package as Nmap:

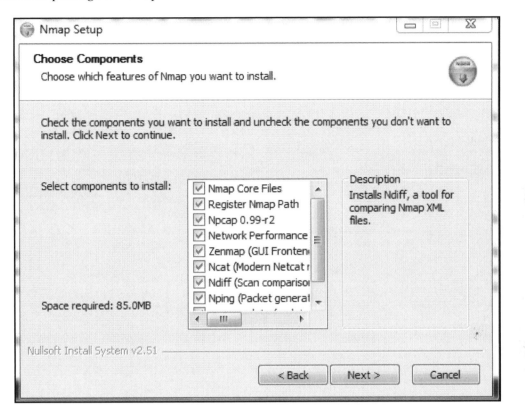

Sometimes, working with command-line tools can be tedious for administrators, thus Zenmap acts as an alternate GUI option.

How do it...

Here are the steps:

1. Open Zenmap from the list of programs.
2. Enter the target to be scanned in the text field provided, as shown here:

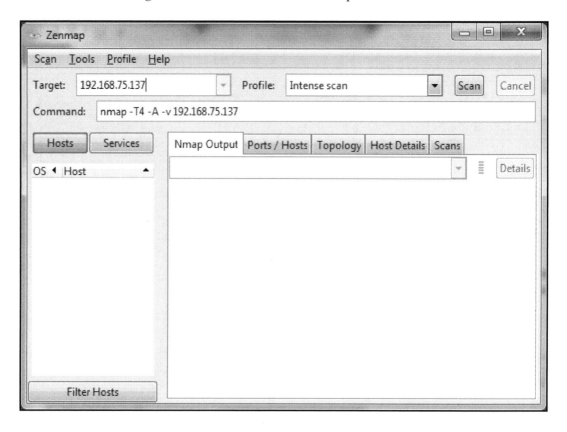

3. Select **Quick scan** from the **Profile** drop-down list, as shown here:

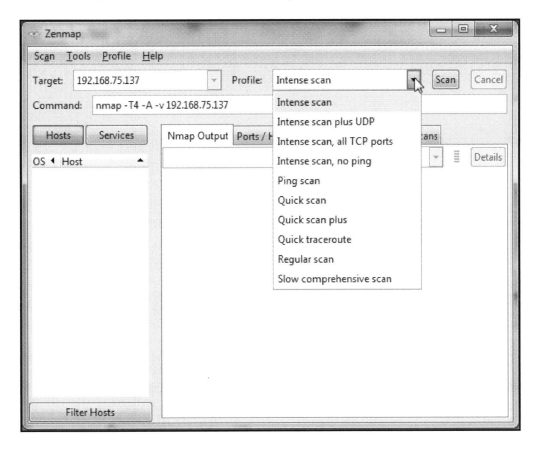

4. This will perform a fast scan with the –F option, thereby giving results for the top 100 ports along with a detailed analysis in different tabs, as shown in the following screenshot:

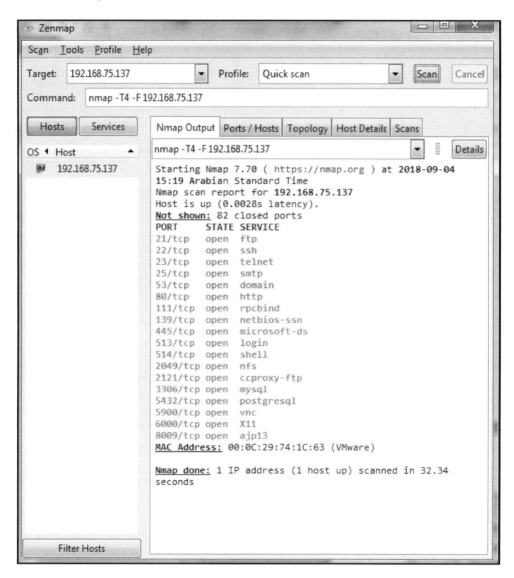

The **Ports/Hosts** tab shows the various open ports along with the services and versions running on them based on the options selected in the scans:

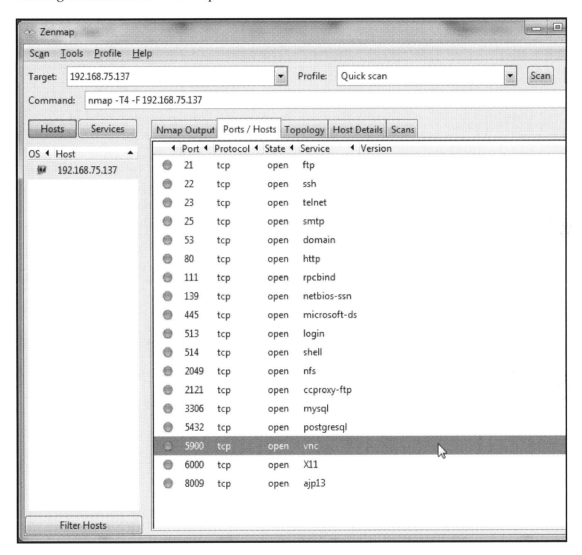

The **Topology** tab shows the network topology detected. This will help an attacker to map the entire network in cases when entire subnets are scanned:

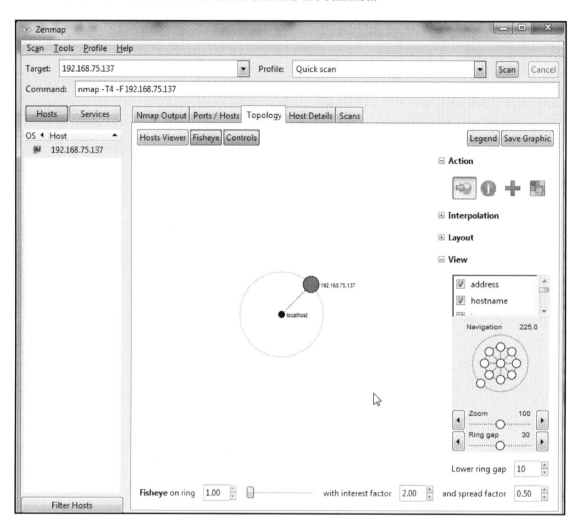

The **Host Details** tab gives information about the MAC address, the state of the host, the number of open and filtered ports, and more:

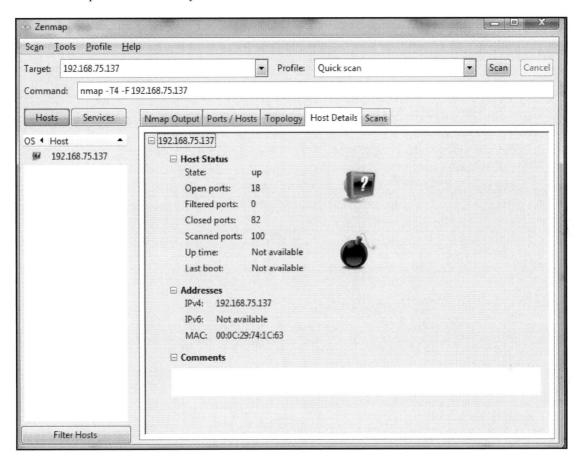

How it works...

Once the user selects the type of scan and the various other options provided by Zenmap and proceeds to scan, the Zenmap interface will call the Nmap engine in the backend to perform similar operations to the command-line interface:

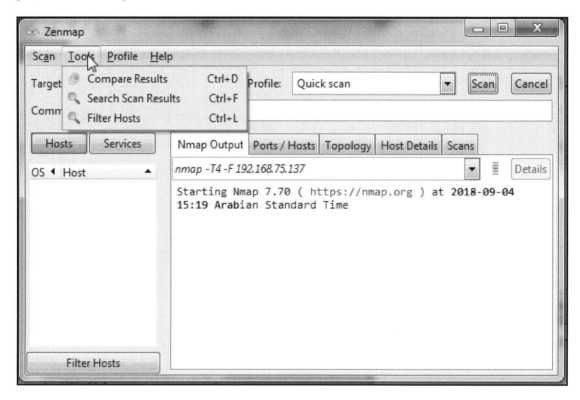

Zenmap also provides various other options to filter the hosts, compare results, search scan results, save scan results, and more.

4
Vulnerability Scanning

In this chapter, we will cover the following recipes:

- How to manage Nessus policies
- How to manage Nessus settings
- How to manage Nessus user accounts
- How to choose a Nessus policy
- How to perform a vulnerability scan using Nessus
- How to manage Nessus scans

Introduction

In this chapter, we will be going through various recipes about how to manage Nessus as a tool and its various components. These recipes will help us gain detailed knowledge of the post-installation steps to be performed in order to be able to configure Nessus to perform network scans of a varied nature.

How to manage Nessus policies

We already learned a great detail about Nessus policies in Chapter 2, *Understanding Network Scanning Tools*. For a quick recap, the Nessus scan policy consists of various settings and content, which is to be used while performing a Network Vulnerability Scan or Compliance Audit. This scan can be created by any Nessus user and can be made available for other users who can then also perform a scan. These policies can be duplicated, imported, and exported based on the user requirements. The only limitation of the policy export is that host-specific data such as Nessus audit files and credential details cannot be exported. These policies are available as part of the resources menu mentioned on the home screen once the user logs in to the Nessus web console:

When a user tries to create a new policy, Nessus provides preexisting scan templates, which can be used to create a new template by customizing the parameters of the scan template:

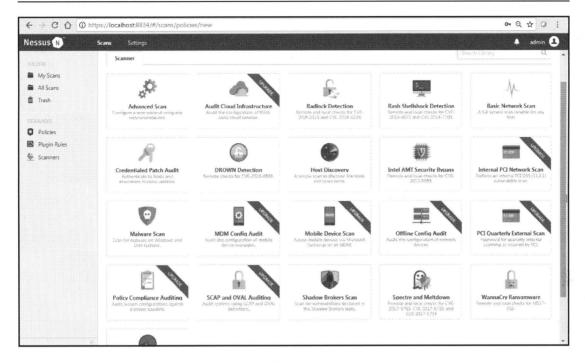

Scan template

Getting ready

In order to perform this activity, you will have to satisfy the following prerequisites on your machine:

- You must have Nessus installed
- You must have network access to the hosts on which the scans are to be performed

In order to install Nesus, you can follow the instructions provided in Chapter 2, *Understanding Network Scanning Tools*. This will allow you to download a compatible version of Nessus and install all the required plugins. In order to check whether your machine has Nessus installed, open the search bar and search for Nessus Web Client. Once found and clicked, this will be opened in the default browser window:

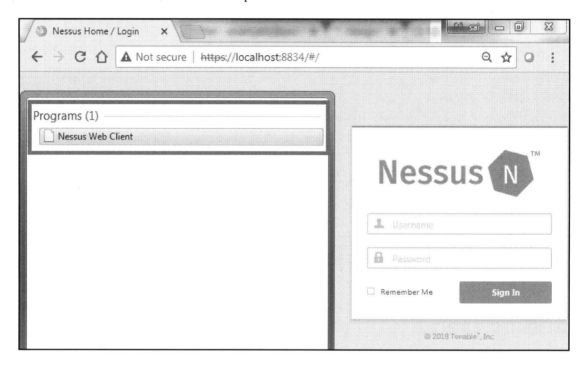

If you are sure about Nessus being correctly installed, you can use the `https://localhost:8834` URL directly from your browser to open the **Nessus Web Client**. If you are unable to locate the Nessus Web Client, you should remove and reinstall Nessus. For the removal of Nessus and installation instructions, refer to `Chapter 2`, *Understanding Network Scanning Tools*. If you have located the Nessus Web Client and are unable to open it in the browser window, you need to check whether the Nessus service is running in the Windows Services utility:

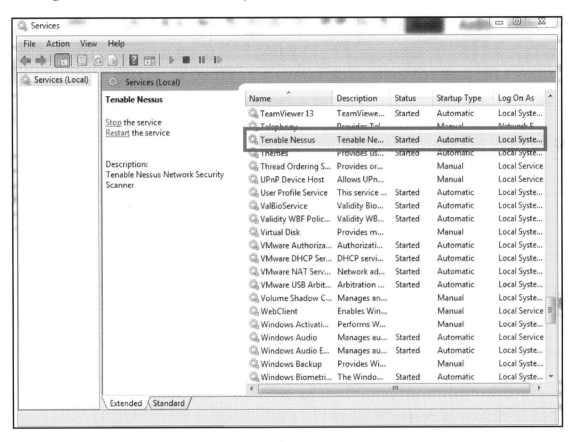

Furthermore, you can start and stop Nessus by using the services utility as per your requirements. In order further to confirm the installation using the command-line interface, you can navigate to the installation directory, where you will be able to see and access Nessus command-line utilities:

```
C:\Windows\system32\cmd.exe

C:\>cd "Program Files"

C:\Program Files>cd Tenable

C:\Program Files\Tenable>cd Nessus

C:\Program Files\Tenable\Nessus>dir
 Volume in drive C has no label.
 Volume Serial Number is B234-0E80

 Directory of C:\Program Files\Tenable\Nessus

16-07-2018  11:45    <DIR>          .
16-07-2018  11:45    <DIR>          ..
16-07-2018  11:45                 1 .winperms
19-06-2018  17:25            45,113 License.rtf
19-06-2018  19:25         6,459,904 nasl.exe
19-06-2018  19:25            46,592 ndbg.exe
19-06-2018  17:25                46 Nessus Web Client.url
19-06-2018  19:22            17,424 nessus-service.exe
19-06-2018  19:25         6,405,120 nessuscli.exe
19-06-2018  19:25         6,837,776 nessusd.exe
               8 File(s)     19,811,976 bytes
               2 Dir(s)   1,970,270,208 bytes free

C:\Program Files\Tenable\Nessus>
```

How to do it...

Perform the following steps:

1. Open the Nessus Web Client.
2. Log in to the Nessus client with the user that you created during installation:

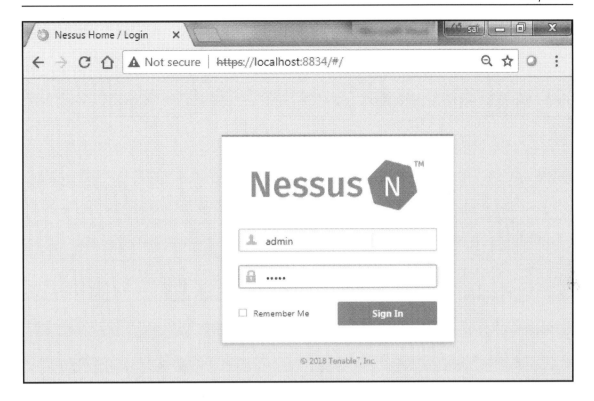

3. Click on the **Policies** option on the left-hand side of the home screen, under **RESOURCES**, to see the **Policies** screen:

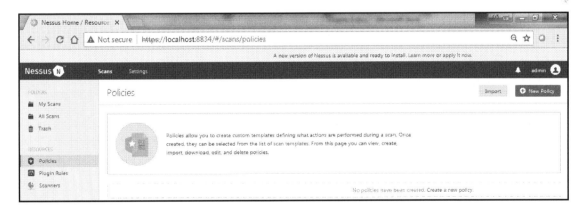

4. Click on **Create a new policy** and on **Basic Network Scan**:

5. Fill in the details for **Name** and **Description**, as follows:

6. Set the group permission to **Can use**.
7. Navigate to the **DISCOVERY** tab and select the type of port scan to be performed from the drop-down:

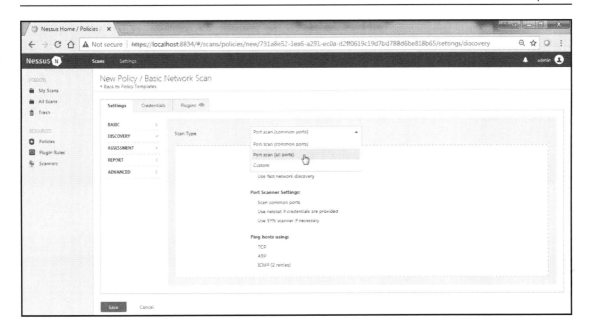

8. Navigate to the **ASSESSMENT** tab and select the type of assessment to be performed from the drop-down:

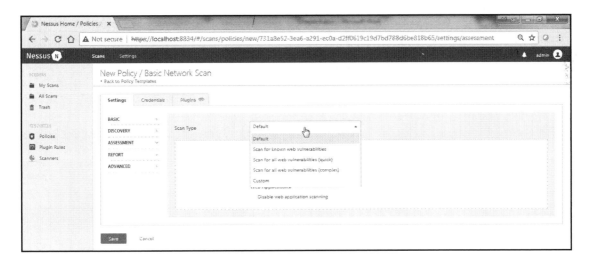

9. Navigate to the **REPORT** tab and select the settings for Nessus to prepare the report as per your requirements:

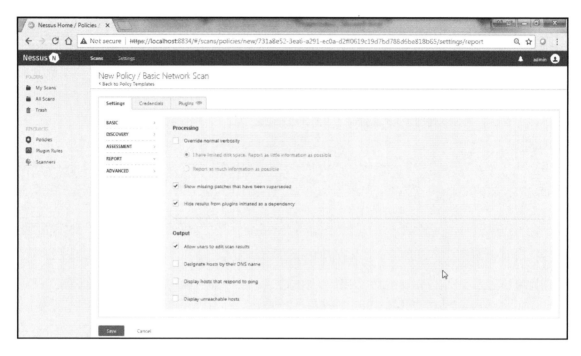

10. Navigate to the **ADVANCED** tab and select the scan settings as per your requirements from the drop-down:

11. If you select **Custom**, a new tab **General** will appear below the **ADVANCED** tab so that you can further customize your scan settings:

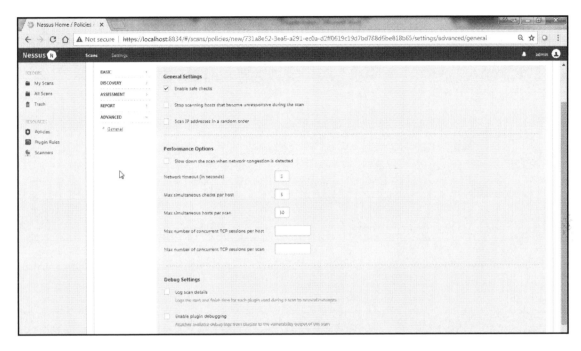

12. Save the scan. This will take you to the **Policies** screen from *Step 2*, which lists the current policy that you created:

13. You can check the checkbox beside the name of the policy and click on the **More** drop-down at the top right to select from the **Copy**, **Export**, and **Delete** options for the policy:

14. Take note of the previous step and click on **Export** to export the policy onto your system:

15. Click on **Export**. A `.nessus` file will have been downloaded onto your system:

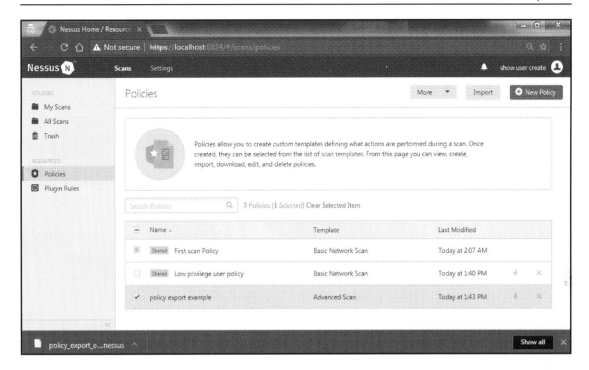

16. In order to import this, click on **Import** and upload the downloaded `.nessus` file:

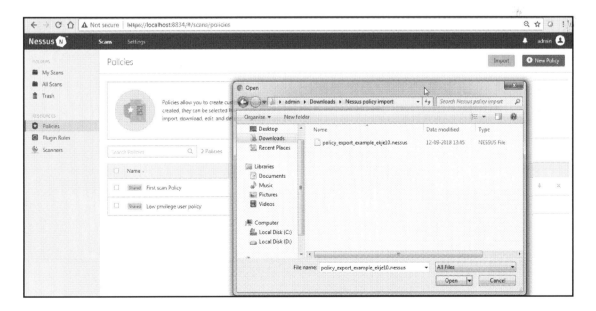

17. The uploaded policy is now visible in the **Policies** screen of the user:

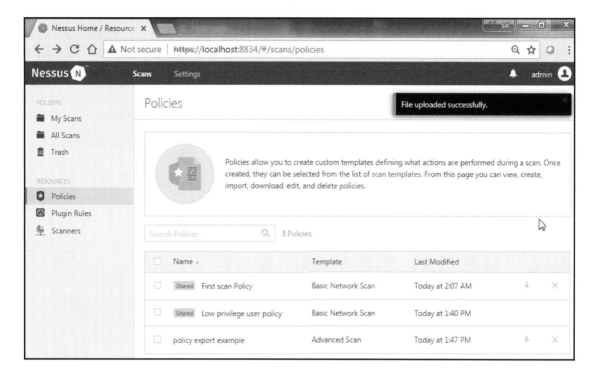

How it works...

The policy that has been created can be used to perform scans by different users. These policies can be imported and exported into another Nessus environment, thus avoiding the creation of new policies.

How to manage Nessus settings

We have already learned a great deal about Nessus settings in Chapter 2, *Understanding Network Scanning Tools*. For a quick recap, in the Nessus settings, we can look at various options available in Nessus. The Nessus settings consist of **About**, **Advanced**, **Proxy Server**, **SMTP Server**, **Custom CA**, and **Password Mgmt**. These menus have further subsettings, which have specific purposes. We will see what can be configured using each menu in the *How to do it...* section.

Getting ready

This section is the same as the *Getting ready* section of the *How to manage Nessus policies* recipe.

How to do it...

Perform the following steps:

1. Open the Nessus Web Client.
2. Log in to the Nessus client with the user that you created during installation.
3. Navigate to the settings screen by clicking on the **Settings** option on the home screen, which directly displays options under the **About** menu:

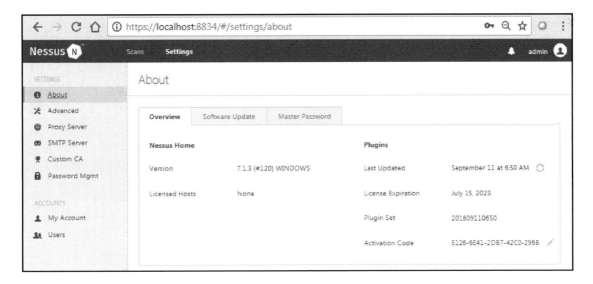

4. Manage the software update settings by navigating to the **Software Update** menu and select the frequency and the type of update you would prefer:

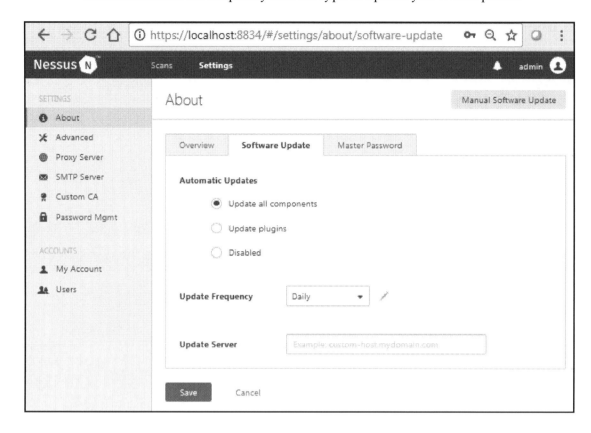

5. Set a master password by navigating to the **Master Password** section to encrypt all the Nessus repositories, policies, results, and configurations:

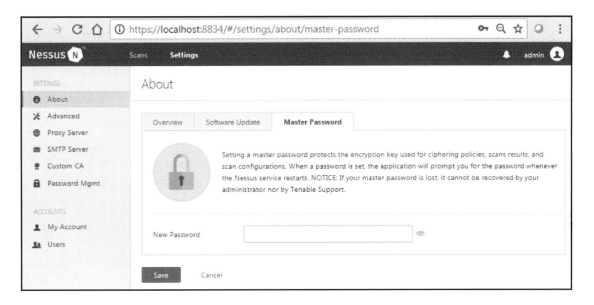

6. Navigate to the **ADVANCED** tab in the left pane under **SETTINGS**. This allows a user to configure 45 different global settings which apply to all the policies and users configured, such as log file, plugin, and path settings:

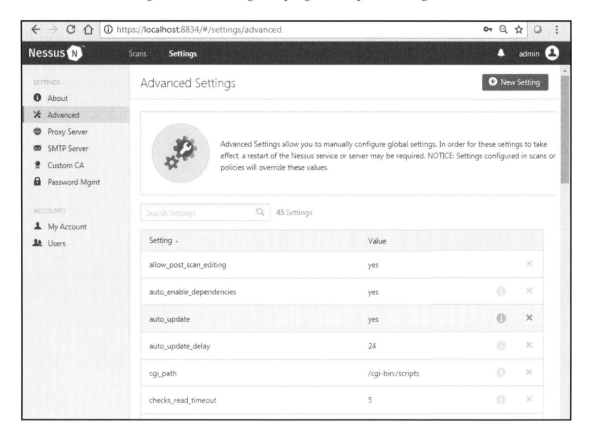

7. Navigate to the **Proxy Server** tab in the left-hand pane under **SETTINGS**. Here, you can configure a proxy server for Nessus to forward the request. This is used when there is a proxy server in-between the host to be scanned and Nessus:

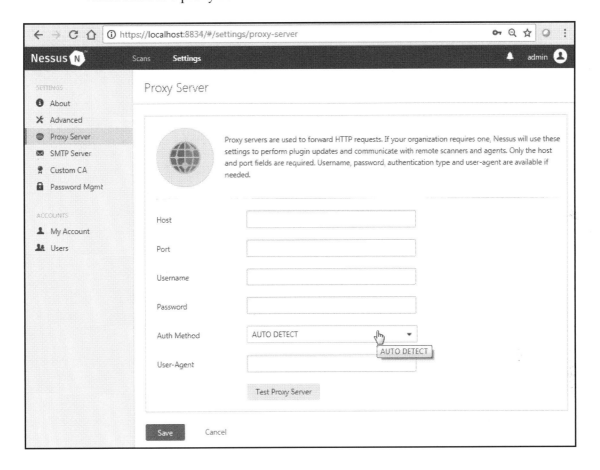

8. Navigate to the **SMTP Server** tab in the left-hand pane under **SETTINGS**. This allows the user to configure SMTP settings for any email notifications the user requires Nessus to send, such as post-scan completion:

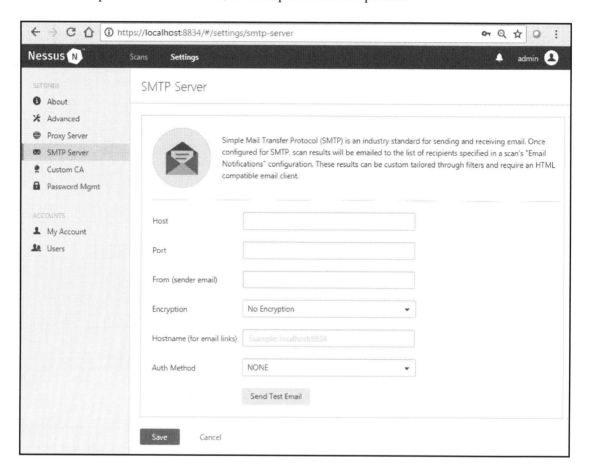

9. Navigate to the **Custom CA** tab in the left-hand pane under **SETTINGS**. Here, the user can upload a custom CA signature, which will be used to avoid false positives in SSL-related findings:

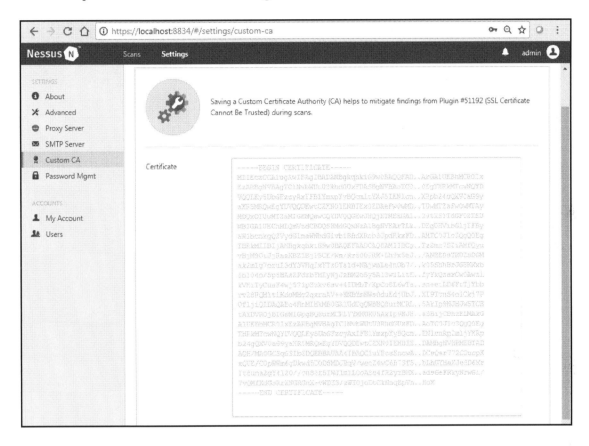

10. Navigate to the **Password Mgmt** tab in the left-hand pane under **SETTINGS**. Here, the admin can configure the password policy to be followed by all the users and groups:

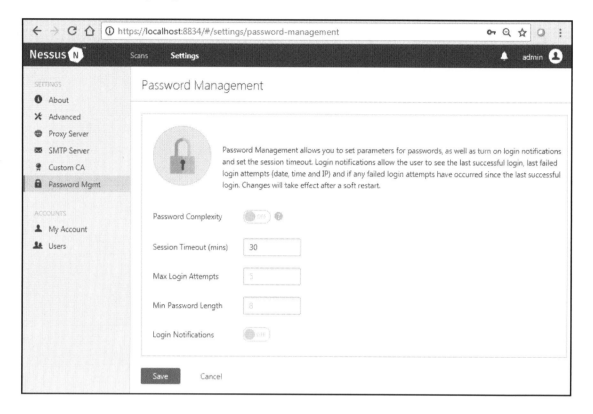

How it works...

These are global settings which are configured for all the users and allow the admin to manage the Nessus console for all the users. These settings are also vital for the functionality of a few features such as email notifications and proxy server configuration.

How to manage Nessus user accounts

Nessus is a multiuser environment, where one admin user can create multiple user accounts and configure global settings, and allow them to configure local policy settings. To be able to use user management, Nessus provides two menu options: **My Account** and **Users**. **My Account** is used to manage your own account and the **Users** tab is used for the admin to manage/create/delete a user. In this recipe, we will see various components of these settings and how one can one use these to manage the Nessus users.

Getting ready

This section is the same as the *Getting ready* section of the *How to manage Nessus policies* recipe.

How to do it...

Perform the following steps:

1. Open the Nessus Web Client.
2. Log in to the Nessus client with the user that you created during installation.

3. Navigate to the **My Account** screen by clicking on the home screen under the **ACCOUNTS** section, which has two sub-options, **Account Settings** and **API Keys**:

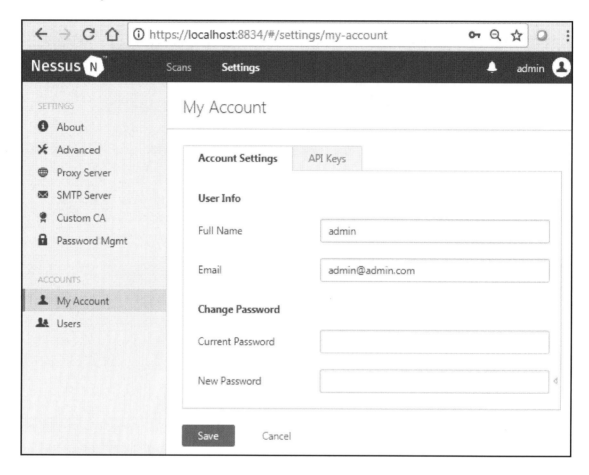

The settings on this page can be used to change the password for the admin user and also set the email ID, which can be used by the email notification feature, and save the settings.

4. Navigate to the **API Keys** tab beside **Account Settings**. Here, you can configure API keys to authenticate with the Nessus rest API. You can create new API keys by clicking the **Generate** button, as follows:

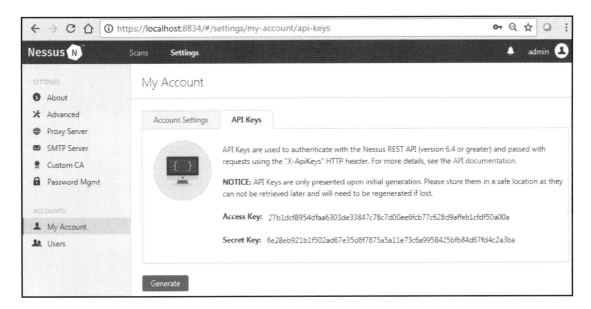

Ensure that you store these keys in a private folder and apply all key-management-related security best practices.

5. Navigate to the **Users** screen by clicking on the home screen under the **ACCOUNTS** section. This will show the users that are currently present in Nessus:

6. Click on **New User** on the top right to create a new user and fill in the details:

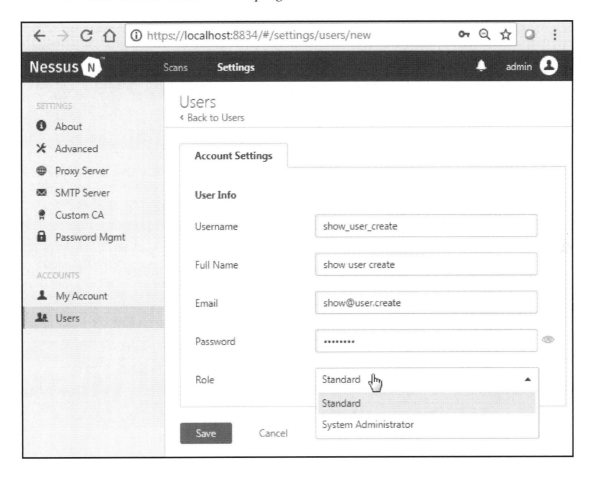

In the preceding screenshot, you can observe that the admin can assign the user role as **Standard** or **System Administrator**. Let's assign the **Standard** role and check the difference between the user privileges:

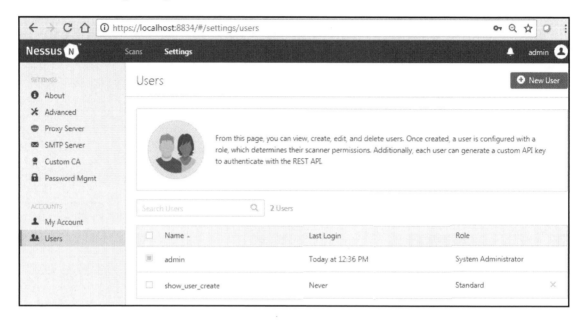

A new user, `show_user_create`, with standard privileges has been created. You can clearly spot the difference in privileges between the users, as shown in the following screenshot. Here, the standard user does not have user creation and account management privileges.

How it works...

User management allows the administrator to create new users and manage their own account. This allows for the segregation of various scans to be performed, instead of having to use one single account to perform all of the scans. This is because Nessus also allows simultaneous login. One account with scans of different users makes it difficult for a user to identify his or her scan at a given point in time, even though they can be moved into different folders.

How to choose a Nessus scan template and policy

Nessus allows a user to customize their scan to the lowest degree, even allowing them to filter the plugins which are to be used, and disable the plugins, which will not be used. Every scan is unique in its own way. For example, if a user wants to perform a credentialed scan, he/she cannot use the host discovery scan template to create a new policy. In order to perform a credentialed scan, the user has to select a basic network scan or an advanced scan which has a feature for the user to enter credentials to authenticate with the machine to be scanned. Thus, it is really important to choose an apt scan template before you create a policy and to choose an apt policy once you create different policies. The second option is to select a previously created template or to import an existing template, which can be used to perform a scan.

The user can also create a policy on the go, just by clicking **New Scan** and selecting an existing template. The only disadvantage of this approach is that you cannot save the policy or the scan template that's used with the custom settings. You will have to create a similar new policy or rescan it using the same host, which will create a history of scans. This creates complications in revisiting the scan for results. In this recipe, we will look into the scan templates that are available in the free version and the policies that can be created by the user.

Getting ready

This section is the same as the *Getting ready* section of the *How to manage Nessus policies* recipe.

How to do it...

Perform the following steps:

1. Open the Nessus Web Client.
2. Log in to the Nessus client with the user that you created during installation.

3. Navigate to the **Policies** tab under the **RESOURCES** section on the home screen. This will list the preexisting policies created by all the users (which are only configured to be shared with everyone):

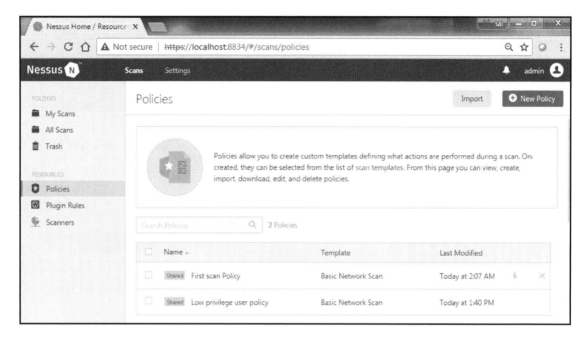

4. You can choose from the existing policies or you can import a policy.

5. If there is no existing policy that satisfies your requirements, you can create a new policy:

   - If a user selects **Advanced Scan**, they can configure every parameter in the policy, thus defining the nature of the policy and whether it should be a network/web application/malware scan. The **ASSESSMENTS** menu makes it unique from other scan templates:

  No other scan template can configure the plugins, except for Advanced Scan.

- The Badlock discovery template allows the user to check whether the remote Windows host is vulnerable to the Samba Badlock vulnerability:

- The **Basic Network Scan** template is used to perform a network-level port scan and identify service-level vulnerabilities with or without credentials for a remote host.
- The credential patch audit scan can be used to check the patch level of the remote host.
- The Drown detection template can be used to detect whether the remote host is vulnerable to a Drown attack:

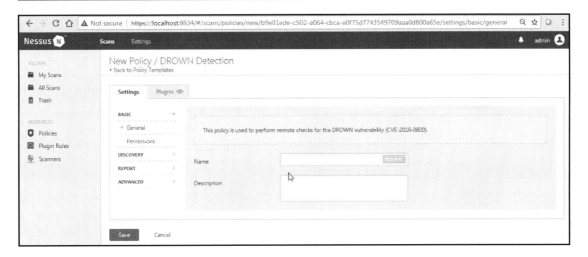

- The host discovery template is used to identify the live hosts from a large range or list of IP addresses, which are provided by the user.
- The **Intel AMT Security Bypass** scan template is used to identify whether the remote host is vulnerable to an Intel AMT Security Bypass:

- The internal PCI network scan template is used to perform an ASV scan on the remote host in order to find out whether the host configuration is PCI-compliant or not.

- The malware scan template is used to perform a malware detection scan on Windows and Unix systems. This is better done when the credentials are provided.
- The policy compliance audit template can be used to perform a baseline configuration audit against an uploaded or preexisting Nessus audit file. We will see this recipe in future chapters.
- The Shadow Brokers Scan template is used to check whether the remote host is vulnerable to the attacks described in the Shadow Broker leaks:

- The Spectre, Meltdown, and WannaCry ransomware templates are used to verify whether those remote host is vulnerable to the respective attacks.
- The web application template is used to perform web application scans that are hosted on the remote host by providing remote HTTP authentication details.

6. Once the specific template is selected, create the policy and save it, as shown in the *How to manage Nessus policies* recipe.

7. Once the policy has been created, it is available for you to select for scanning under the user-created policies section of the **Policies** screen from the **New Scan** task:

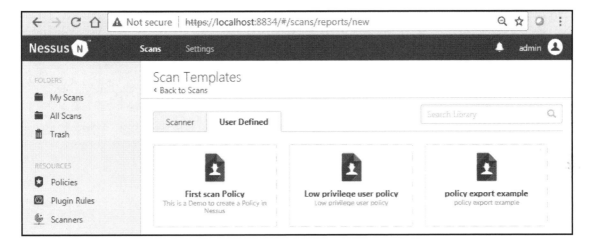

8. You can also select the policy on the go while creating a new scan by selecting the template and filling in the details.

How it works...

In order to perform a scan correctly, it is equally important to select an apt policy. This will help the user to obtain correct results and saves a lot of time when confirming and reporting the vulnerabilities. For example, if a user wants to know the open ports and he or she goes to perform an advanced scan, he/she will obtain results for configuration audit, patch audit, and many unnecessary plugins which were used in the scan. Instead, if the user had selected a basic network scan, all he/she would find would be open ports and a list of vulnerabilities affecting the services running on those hosts.

How to perform a vulnerability scan using Nessus

From following the preceding recipes, a user should be able to understand the creation and selection of a policy. Once the policy has been decided upon, all the user needs to do is to identify the host to be scanned, select the policy, and click Scan. The general scan time for Nessus for a noncredential scan of a single host with few ports open will take a couple of minutes. As the number of hosts and ports keeps increasing, the time required for the scan also becomes high.

 It is always recommended to inform the stakeholders before performing a Nessus scan, as it would allow an overhead of incident investigation on whether an attack was performed on the host and also inform network admins as to whether network bandwidth utilization may be higher than it is normally.

Getting ready

This section is the same as the *Getting ready* section of the *How to manage Nessus policies* recipe. This recipe will also require the user to have studied the previous recipes in this chapter.

How to do it...

Perform the following steps:

1. Open the Nessus Web Client.
2. Log in to the Nessus client with the user that you created during installation.
3. Click on **Create a new scan**.

4. Select the **Basic Network Scan** template and fill in the required details for the scan, such as **Name**, **Description**, remote host for scanning, and leave the credentials blank for a noncredential scan:

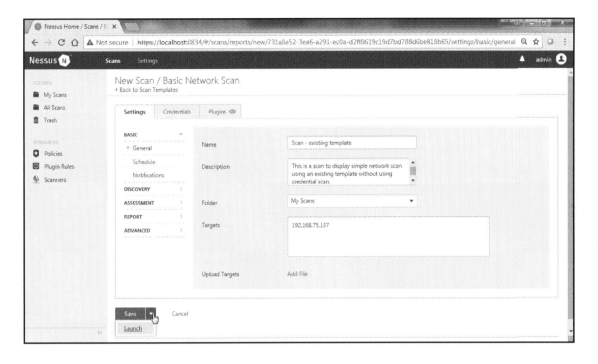

You can enter the hosts to be scanned in newline or separated by commas. You can also upload a list of the hosts to be scanned:

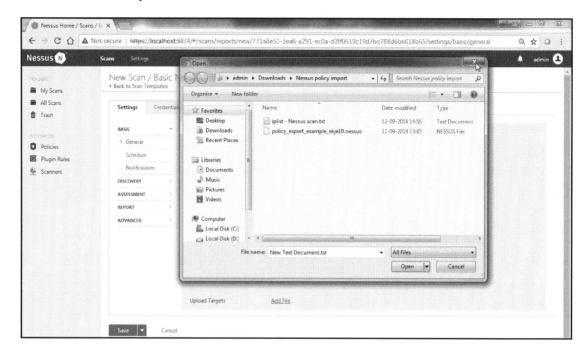

You can also schedule the scan for a future time and date by enabling the configuration options in the **Schedule** menu:

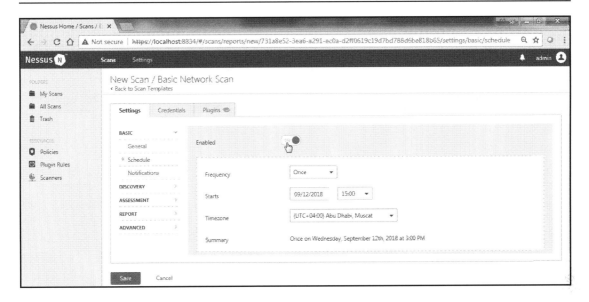

5. Launch the scan:

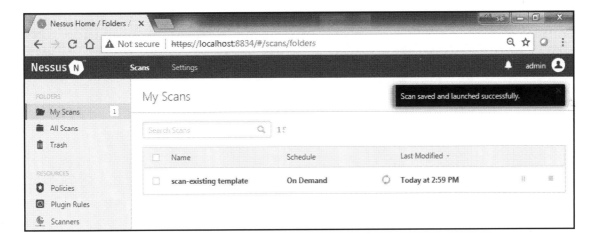

6. Open the scan to see the results once the scan has completed:

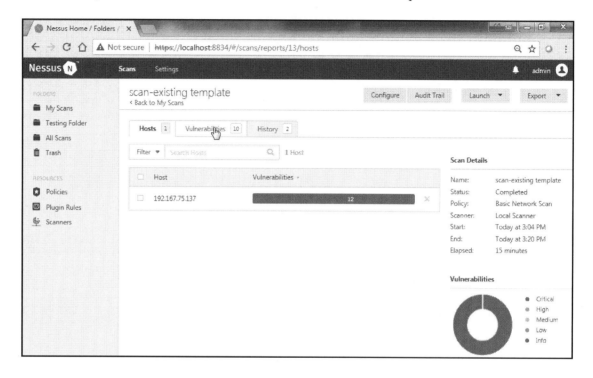

Furthermore, to see the name of the vulnerabilities, you can click on the bar or the **Vulnerabilities** tab:

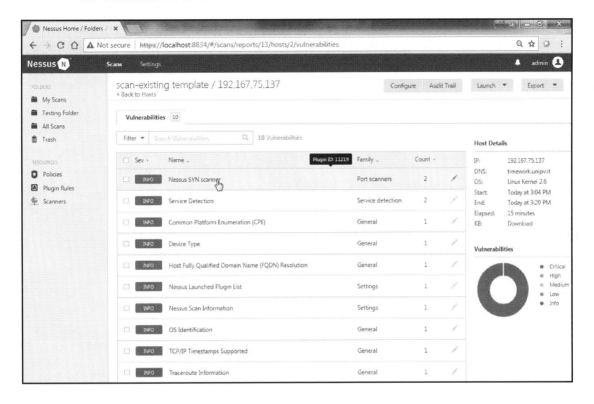

7. Select the **Basic Network Scan** template and fill in the required details for the scan such as **Name**, **Description**, remote host for scanning, along with the credentials for a credential scan:

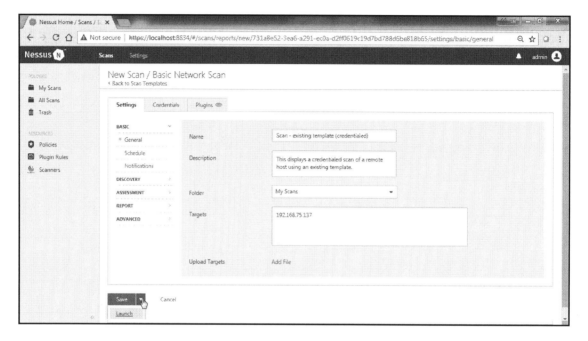

We will enter the credentials for password-based SSH authentication, as the host is a Linux platform. Nessus also supports Windows-based authentication:

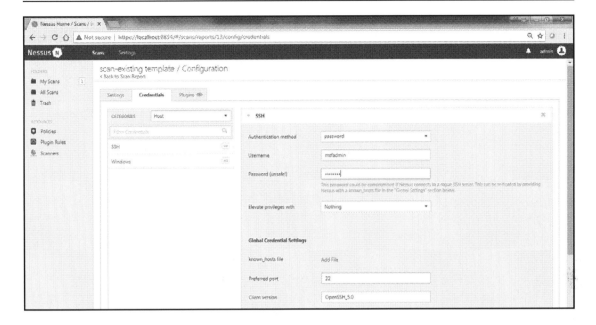

8. Launch the scan:

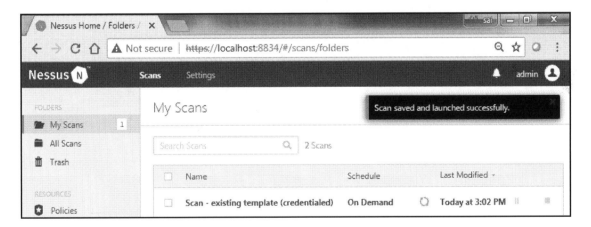

9. Open the scan to see the results once the scan has completed:

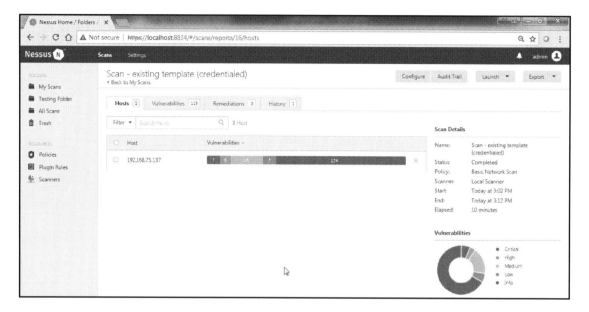

Furthermore, to see the name of the vulnerabilities, you can click on the bar or the **Vulnerabilities** tab:

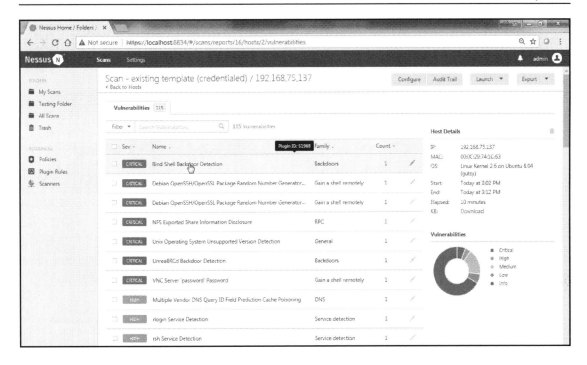

Nessus also provides separate tabs for specific remediations that should be mentioned by Nessus. You can also look at the scan history:

10. If the scan was not performed as per your requirements, you don't perform the whole scan again. Instead, you can use the **Configure** option on the top right of the scan result page to reconfigure the scan settings and launch a fresh scan:

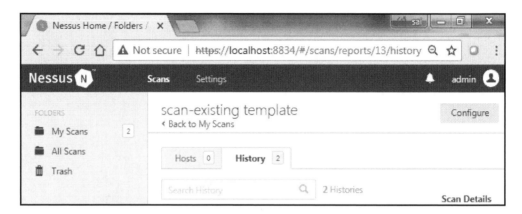

11. This will create a history of scans being performed using the same template. You can click on the respective scan for which you want to see the results from the history, and thus obtain the scan results:

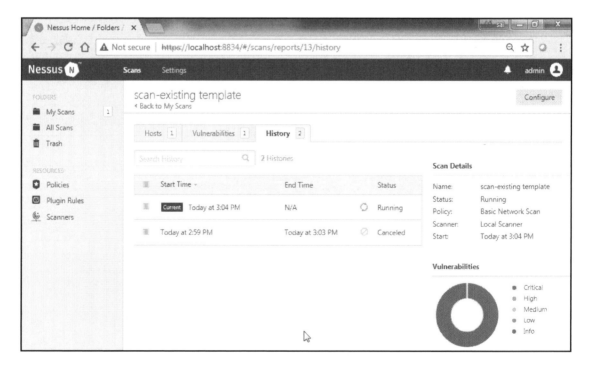

Similarly, you can perform a scan using user-defined policies by selecting the **User Defined** template on the new scan screen:

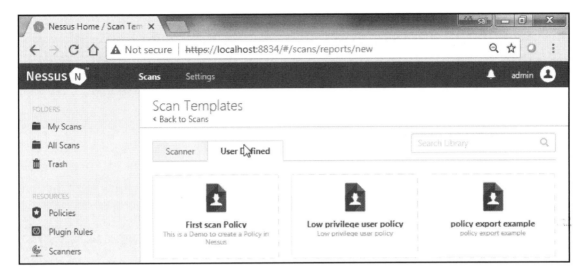

You can export the report for the scan that has been performed into different formats that are available in Nessus by selecting the respective format from the drop-down. We will look at reporting further in the chapters that follow.

How it works...

Nessus scan has various options such as credentialed, noncredentialed, compliance audit, and ASV scan. By performing these automated scans, a simple network engineer will be able to determine the security posture of the organization's IT infrastructure.

How to manage Nessus scans

Once performed, Nessus scans can be further segregated into folders to avoid different scans being clustered together. This also allows the auditor easy access to the results. A user can create/delete/move/copy the scans on Nessus. In this recipe, we will be looking at various operations that a user can perform on a completed Nessus scan.

Getting ready

This section is the same as the *Getting ready* section of the *How to manage Nessus policies* recipe. This recipe will also require that the user has studied and completed the previous recipes in this chapter.

How to do it...

Perform the following steps:

1. Open the Nessus Web Client.
2. Log in to the Nessus client with the user that you created during installation.
3. You can create a new folder by using the **New Folder** option on the top right of the home screen:

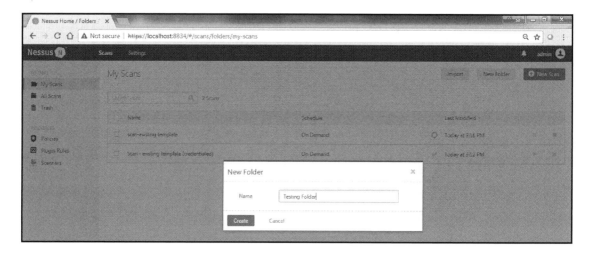

4. Once the new folder has been created, a user can navigate into the folder and create a **New Scan** so that the results are populated in that folder and do not appear on the home screen:

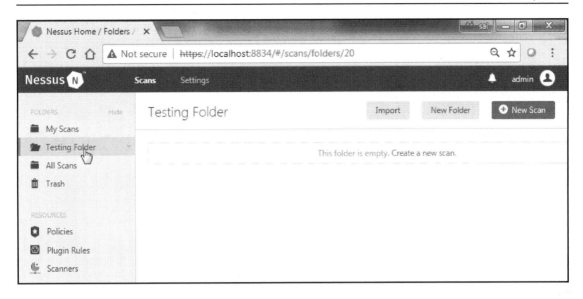

5. You can also copy or move an existing completed scan to the created folder by selecting the scan and clicking on the **Move to folder** option on the top right corner of the Nessus home screen:

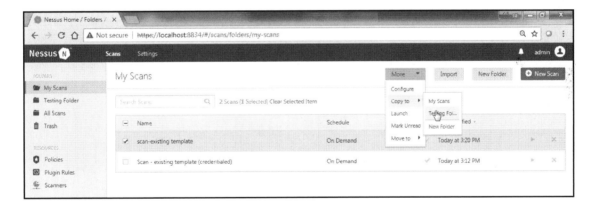

This will create a copy of the scan in the folder by keeping the main scan report on the home screen:

6. Scan the copy created in the `Testing Folder`:

Moving the scan to the `Testing Folder` will delete the scan from the home screen and move the original to the folder:

Now, you can delete the scan that was moved to the `Testing Folder`:

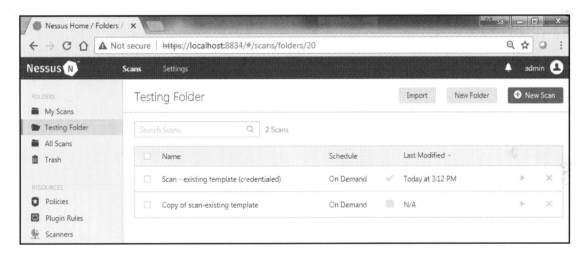

7. You can also delete scans by selecting the specific scan and moving it to the trash:

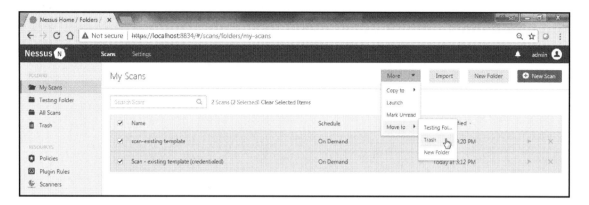

How it works...

Sorting Nessus scans can become a tedious task when there are a number of scan results lying in your default Nessus folder. Instead, the preceding options will help a user to segregate Nessus scans and maintain folders so that they can access the results on the go.

Configuration Audits

5

In this chapter, we will cover the following:

- Introducing compliance scans
- Selecting a compliance scan policy
- Introducing configuration audits
- Performing an operating system audit
- Performing a database audit
- Performing a web application scan

Introducing compliance scans

In this chapter, we will be going through various recipes on the significance of Nessus for performing various audits, such as a credentialed scan, and performing policy compliance audits, such as an operating system audit, a database audit, and an application audit. This is a crucial part of a white box assessment for network security, as this allows an internal administrator or auditor to understand the security posture of the systems in the organization.

Selecting a compliance scan policy

An entire compliance scan or audit is different from a typical vulnerability scan; it is completely dependent on the plugins and the Nessus audit file. We have already covered the basics on how to download and update the plugins in Chapter 2, *Understanding Network Scanning Tools*. We will now uncover further details about plugins and the Nessus audit file. In this recipe, we will look how to select the correct baseline policy from the set of policies that come preloaded in Nessus, in order to perform a configuration audit for a Linux host.

Plugins

Each plugin consists of syntax to check for a specific vulnerability for a version or multiple versions of the software, services, and operating systems. A group of plugins for a similar operating system/service/software are grouped as a plugin family, shown as follows:

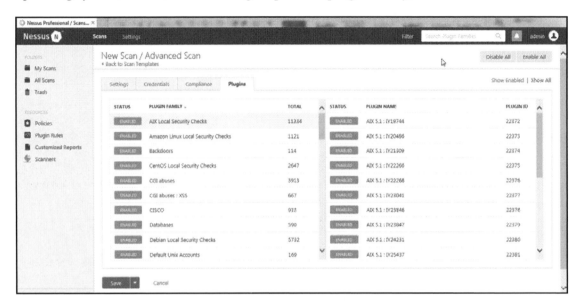

These plugin families expand into different plugins that each perform a specific check. A user cannot manually add a plugin; they can only download or update new or missing plugins only when they are made available by Tenable. Each plugin has a set of parameters to help a user understand the plugin. These parameters are discussed in greater detail in the following section.

Synopsis

This section consists of brief information about the vulnerability and acts as a title for the vulnerability.

Description

This section provides deeper insight into the vulnerability of the exact component and version (if available) affected, along with details about the vulnerability. This allows the user to understand which part of the service or software is vulnerable, and the vulnerability as a whole.

Solution

This section provides the user with details of remediation, such as configuration changes or code changes that are to be performed, or a link to an article by Tenable or any other trusted source on how to mitigate the vulnerability.

Plugin information

This section consists of parameters that differentiate the plugin from other plugins. Parameters include the ID, version, type, publication date, and modified date. These parameters act as metadata for the plugin.

Risk information

This section provides information about the severity of the vulnerability, alongside **Common Vulnerability Scoring System (CVSS)** data, which is one of the globally accepted standards for scoring vulnerabilities. The severity ratings vary from Critical to Informational; the CVSS score is on a scale of 1-10.

Vulnerability information

This section provides details about the platform for which the plugin is applicable, using the **Common Platform Enumeration (CPE)** index, which is currently maintained by the **National Vulnerability Database (NVD)**. Further, it also provides information about the exploitability of the vulnerability, using parameters such as exploit available and exploit ease. It also consists of the publication date of the plugin.

Reference information

This section consists of information about reference IDs assigned to the vulnerability sent to the plugin by various known bodies, such as NVD and Secunia. These references include EDB-ID, BID, Secunia, and CVE-ID.

Each plugin, plugin family, or even all plugins, can be enabled and disabled as per the user's requirements, thus allowing the user to reduce the scan time and use only the necessary plugins to perform a scan. The following screenshot shows a single plugin disabled:

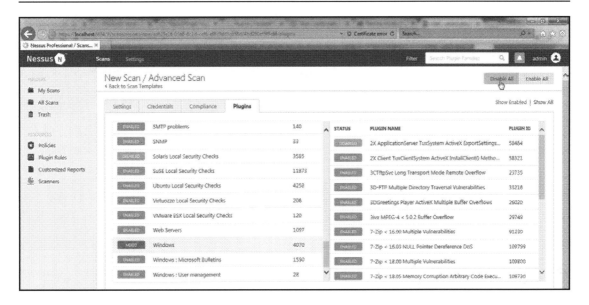

The following screenshot shows a whole plugin family disabled:

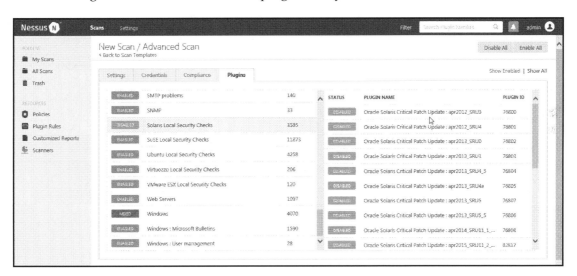

The following screenshot shows all the plugins disabled, using the **Disable All** button at the top right of the screen:

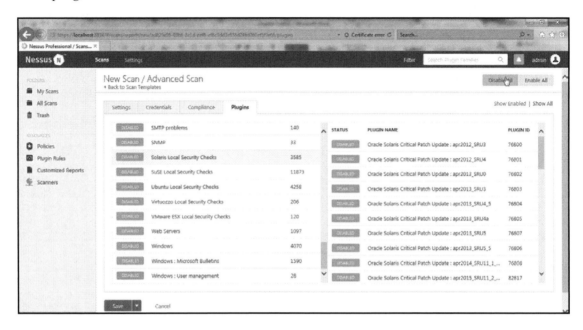

The very important components of the plugins needed to perform the compliance scan are the policy compliance plugins. These plugins will be used along with the audit file provided to identify the operating system-level, service-level, and configuration-level vulnerabilities. For example, if you want to perform a compliance scan for Windows, you can disable all the remaining plugins and enable only **Windows Compliance Checks**, as follows:

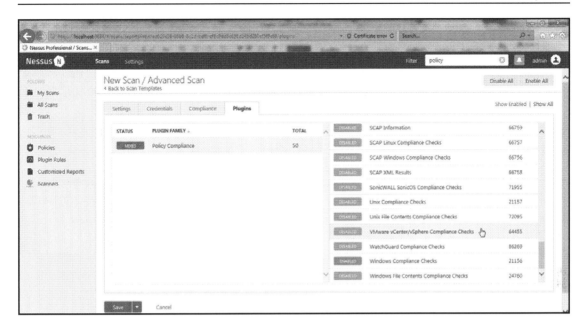

Compliance standards

There are many standards in different sectors that have to be followed, and to which organizations are required to be compliant, in order to perform certain business operations or to ensure the security of their information. For example, most payment gateways, or any payment-related functionality, are required to be tested against the PCI standard to be considered secure.

The following are some of the standards in the market to which relevant organizations are expected to be compliant:

- ETSI **Cybersecurity technical committee (TC CYBER)**
- ISO/IEC 27001 and 27002
- CISQ
- DoCRA
- NERC
- NIST

- ISO 15408
- RFC 2196
- ANSI/ISA 62443 (formerly ISA-99)
- The **ISA Security Compliance Institute (ISCI)** Conformity Assessment Program
- ISCI Certification offerings
- ISO 17065 and Global Accreditation
- Chemical, oil, and gas industries
- IEC 62443
- IEC 62443 Certification programs
- IASME
- Banking Regulators

Auditors create a checklist to identify the gaps against an industry standard baseline, thus allowing the organization to work on filling in the gaps to become compliant and certified. The compliance module in Nessus works in a similar fashion. It works to identify configuration gaps, data leakage, and compliance against various benchmarks.

The Nessus compliance module provides default audit files to check compliance against benchmarks for operating systems, network devices, software, and services running. Nessus has preloaded audit files for the **Center for Internet Security (CIS)**, **Health Insurance Portability and Accountability Act (HIPAA)**, and **Tenable Network Security (TNS)**. It also allows the user to write a custom audit file using **Nessus Attack Scripting Language (NASL)**. We will look at the customization of this in Chapter 7, *Understanding the Customization and Optimization of Nessus and Nmap*.

Getting ready

In order to perform this activity, you will have to satisfy the following prerequisites on your machine:

- Installing Nessus
- Getting network access to the hosts on which the scans are to be performed

In order to install Nesus, you can follow the instructions provided in Chapter 2, *Understanding Network Scanning Tools*. This will allow you to download a compatible version of Nessus and install all the required plugins. In order to check whether your machine has Nessus installed on it already, open the search bar and search for the Nessus Web Client. Once found and clicked on, this will be opened in the default browser window:

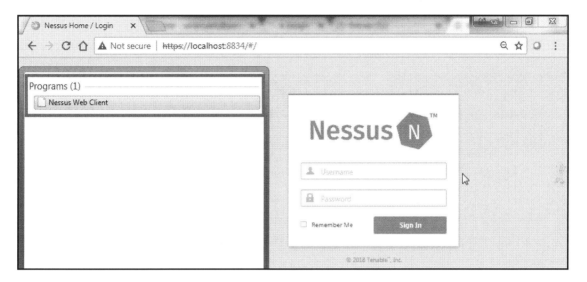

If you are sure Nessus is correctly installed, you can use the `https://localhost:8834` URL directly in your browser to open the Nessus Web Client. If you are unable to locate the Nessus Web Client, you should remove and re-install Nessus. For the removal of Nessus and installation instructions, refer to `chapter 2`, *Understanding Network Scanning Tools*. If you have located the Nessus Web Client and are unable to open it in the browser window, you need to check whether the Nessus service is running in the Windows services utility, as shown here:

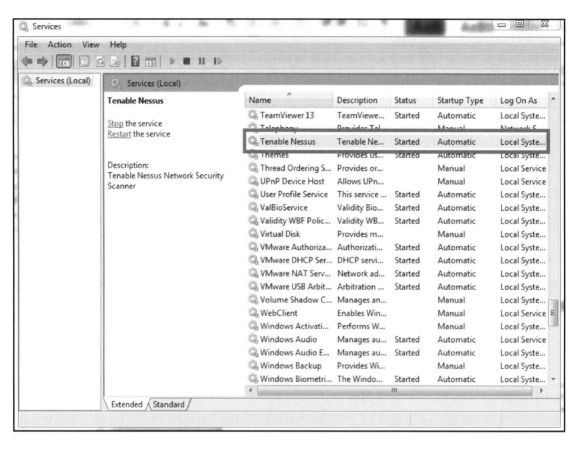

You can also start and stop Nessus as per your requirements by using the services utility. In order to further confirm the installation using the command-line interface, you can navigate to the installation directory to see and access Nessus command-line utilities:

```
C:\Windows\system32\cmd.exe

C:\>cd "Program Files"

C:\Program Files>cd Tenable

C:\Program Files\Tenable>cd Nessus

C:\Program Files\Tenable\Nessus>dir
 Volume in drive C has no label.
 Volume Serial Number is B234-0E80

 Directory of C:\Program Files\Tenable\Nessus

16-07-2018  11:45    <DIR>          .
16-07-2018  11:45    <DIR>          ..
16-07-2018  11:45                 1 .winperms
19-06-2018  17:25            45,113 License.rtf
19-06-2018  19:25         6,459,904 nasl.exe
19-06-2018  19:25            46,592 ndbg.exe
19-06-2018  17:25                46 Nessus Web Client.url
19-06-2018  19:22            17,424 nessus-service.exe
19-06-2018  19:25         6,405,120 nessuscli.exe
19-06-2018  19:25         6,837,776 nessusd.exe
               8 File(s)     19,811,976 bytes
               2 Dir(s)   1,970,270,208 bytes free

C:\Program Files\Tenable\Nessus>
```

It is always recommended to have administrator or root-level credentials to provide the scanner access to all system files. This will allow the scanner to perform a deeper scan and populate better results compared to a non-credentialed scan. The policy compliance module is only available in paid versions of Nessus, such as Nessus Professional or Nessus Manager. For these, you will have to purchase an activation key from Tenable and update it in the **Settings** page, as shown here:

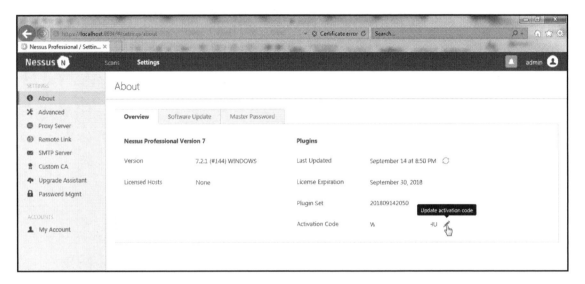

Click on the **Edit** button to open a window and enter the new activation code purchased from Tenable:

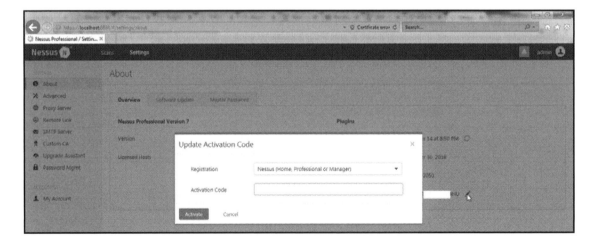

In order to test the scans, we need to install a virtual machine. In order to run a virtual machine, I would recommend using VMware, which can be downloaded and installed from `https://www.vmware.com/products/workstation-pro/workstation-pro-evaluation.html`.

For the test system, readers can download Metasploitable (a vulnerable virtual machine by Rapid 7) from `https://information.rapid7.com/download-metasploitable-2017.html`. Apply the following steps to open Metasploitable. This provides various components, including an operating system, a database, and a vulnerable application, which will help us to test the recipes in the current chapter:

1. Unzip the downloaded **Metasploitable** package:

Metasploitable.nvram	04-09-2018 16:53	NVRAM File	9 KB
Metasploitable.vmdk	17-09-2018 13:48	VMware virtual dis...	18,81,024 KB
Metasploitable.vmsd	07-05-2010 14:46	VMSD File	0 KB
Metasploitable.vmx	17-09-2018 13:47	VMware virtual m...	3 KB
Metasploitable.vmxf	07-05-2010 14:46	VMXF File	1 KB

2. Open the `.vmx` file using the installed VMware Workstation or VMware Player:

3. Log in using `msfadmin`/`msfadmin` as the username and password:

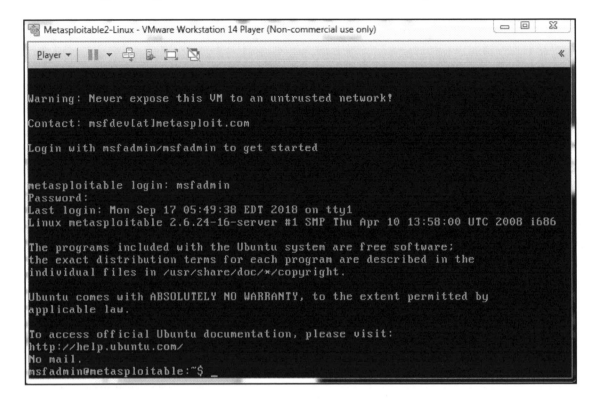

Chapter 5

How do it...

Perform the following steps:

1. Open the Nessus Web Client.
2. Log in to the Nessus Web Client with the user info created during installation.
3. Click on the **Policies** tab and select **Create a new policy**.
4. Select **Advanced Scan** and fill in the required details:

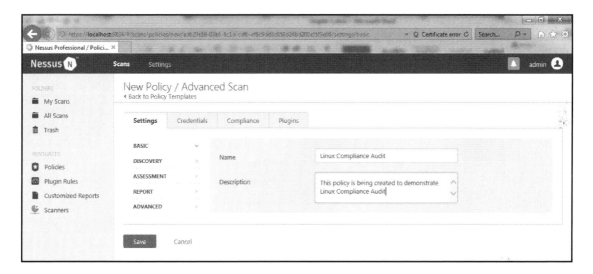

5. Navigate to the **Compliance** tab and search for Linux benchmarks available in Nessus:

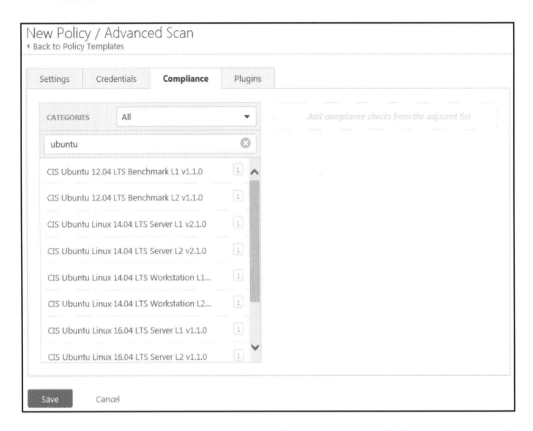

This shows various benchmarks for different versions of Ubuntu. But in order to select the appropriate profile, we will first have to identify the version of Ubuntu running on the test machine.

6. Use the `lsb_release -a` command on the test machine to display the version of Ubuntu running:

```
msfadmin@metasploitable:~$ lsb_release -a
No LSB modules are available.
Distributor ID: Ubuntu
Description:    Ubuntu 8.04
Release:        8.04
Codename:       hardy
msfadmin@metasploitable:~$
msfadmin@metasploitable:~$
```

It is clear that the remote test machine is running on Ubuntu 8.04, hence we will have to select the lowest available version in the available audit files to obtain approximate results.

7. Select the **CIS Benchmark** file for **Ubuntu 12.04**, as it is the lowest version available:

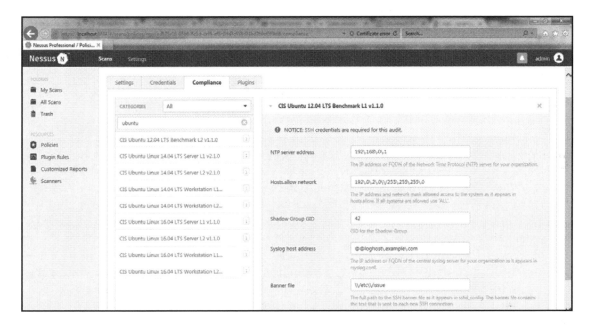

You can choose to change the available parameters, such as **NTP server address**, **Hosts.allow network**, **Shadow Group ID**, **Syslog host address**, and **Banner file** location, if there is any specific server/location to be configured. Also, as shown in the preceding screenshot, the SSH credentials for the remote Ubuntu host have to be entered.

How it works...

Selecting an appropriate Nessus file is very important for performing any compliance scan, as the underlying syntax in NASL is customized for every audit file as per the operating system chosen. A Windows audit file would not work on Linux, and vice versa. To ensure that the right policy is selected, it is always recommend to check the operating system version to the last decimal point and select the policy for the closest available decimal.

Introducing configuration audits

A configuration audit is an information security procedure where you prepare a baseline configuration, and then compare this with the current configuration to perform a gap analysis, later working on closing those gaps to get as close as possible to the baseline configuration. This process of closing the gaps and achieving a maximum hardened state is called risk or vulnerability mitigation.

Most companies and organizations rely on strong configurations to ensure security in their systems. A well hardened and patched system is a nightmare for a hacker to break into. As many companies opt to move their operations to the cloud, configuration plays a great role in security now more than ever. A simple lapse in a network device, allowing default users to log in, would help a hacker gain access to a whole network in minutes.

A regular application has two major components: the frontend and the backend. The frontend is where the end users access the application as a visible resource. Anything that is not visible or not accessible to the end user, then, can be considered the backend. This includes the web server, application server, database server, router, firewall, and intrusion prevention and detection systems. All of these devices could be physically different or being handled by a single cluster of servers. All of these are software that can be installed on any physical server; that is, an Apache Web Server can be installed on a normal computer with the Windows operating system. A simple XAMPP package installs a web/app server, a database, and an application framework. All these different components come with different configurations—a simple misconfiguration at any level of the application architecture can compromise the security of the whole system:

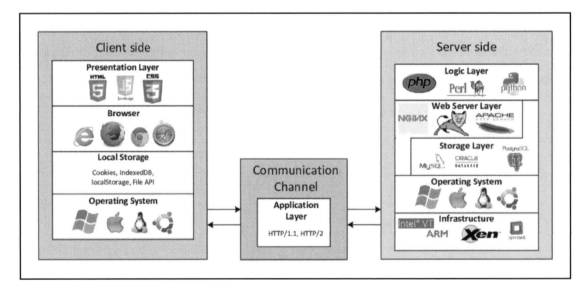

A configuration audit will ensure that the structure of any organization's network security will be strengthened. Continuous monitoring of the changes to configurations of network devices and services in the infrastructure also helps to ensure safe configuration of the devices and servers. The following are some of the steps that can be taken to ensure strict hardening of servers:

1. Detecting any dynamic changes in the configuration
2. Configuration audit on new or changed configurations should be performed
3. Examining device and server logs strictly
4. Audit is to be performed on end-end of the network right from web application to the database

There are four major types of audits that can be performed during the configuration audit, as discussed in the following sections.

Database audit

As a part of the database audit, it is recommended to perform an audit on the database configuration, schema, users, privileges, and structures. A baseline can be created by using the secure configuration guides produced by the respective manufacturer, and analyzing the gaps present in the configuration. Some of the sample database configuration checks are as follows:

- Authentication methods
- Revoking unnecessary privileges and roles from the role public
- Restricting permissions on runtime facilities
- Ensuring that TCPs are specified as the PROTOCOL in the ADDRESS parameter in the tnsnames.ora file

Network device audit

As a part of the network configuration audit, it is recommended to perform an audit on firewall configuration, the firewall rulebase, router configuration, web application firewall signatures, and email client configuration. These are essential components in any network, as one faulty rule in the firewall could expose the whole network to the internet. The following are some of the checks to be performed on network devices:

- Authentication methods
- Access control list review
- Communication security

Operating system audit

As a part of an operating system audit, it is always recommended to audit access control, security settings, errors reports, a password policy, and folder permissions. These checks will fall in the same category, more or less, except for the actual method to obtain and audit the operating system. The following are some of the operating system checks to be performed:

- Authentication methods
- Password policy
- Partition and data segregation
- Public shares

Application audit

An application audit is one of the major components to be performed in a configuration and compliance audit. Instead of simply checking for configuration uses, it is always recommended to hunt for security bugs in the application caused by poorly built modules and services; for example, an application module allowing user input directly into SQL queries without any sanitization. This could allow an attacker with basic knowledge of SQL to craft queries and dump the entire database without having any network-level access directly to the database. It is very important for everyone to understand the significance of end-to-end security.

The following are the top 10 most critical web application security risks, as listed by OWASP:

- Injection
- Broken authentication
- Sensitive data exposure
- **XML external entities** (**XXE**)
- Broken access control
- Security misconfiguration
- **Cross-site scripting** (**XSS**)
- Insecure deserialization
- Using components with known vulnerabilities
- Insufficient logging and monitoring

Performing an operating system audit

In the previous recipes, we have learned a great deal about the need for configuration audits and their contribution toward more secure networks. In this recipe, we will be looking at using the compliance scan feature of Nessus to perform a configuration audit of an operating system.

Getting ready

The *Getting ready* section for this recipe is same as the *Getting ready* section of the *Selecting a compliance scan policy* section. This recipe will also require you to have studied and practiced the previous recipes in this chapter.

How do it...

Perform the following steps:

1. Open the Nessus Web Client.
2. Log in to the Nessus Web Client with the user details created during installation.
3. Follow the steps from the *Selecting a compliance scan policy* recipe.
4. Navigate to the **Credentials** tab and select **SSH** credentials to be entered, as it is a Ubuntu test system. Select password-based authentication and fill in the **Username** and **Password (unsafe!)** fields, as shown here:

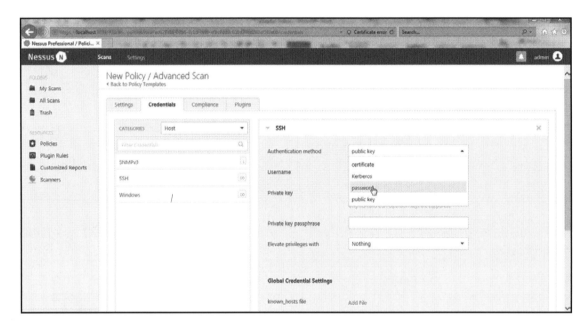

If you have remote root login disabled in any Linux system, you can log in as a low privilege user and elevate to root privilege, as Nessus provides an **Elevate privileges with** option. All you have to do is select **Root** from the drop-down menu and enter the root password. Nessus will log in as the low-privilege user and run an `su` command in the background to log in using `root`:

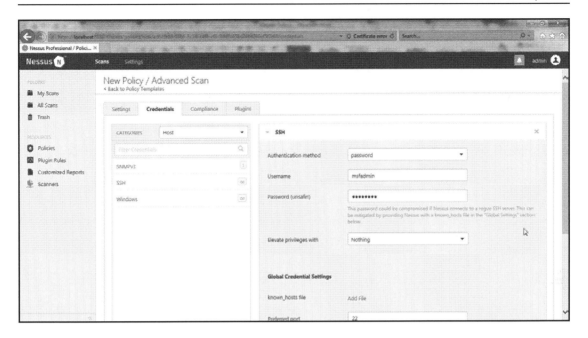

5. Now navigate to the **Plugins** tab and enable only the plugins required for this scan—as mentioned earlier in the book, this reduces scan time and provides quicker results:

6. Then save the policy, as shown here:

7. Navigate to **Scans** and select **New Scan**, and click on **User Defined** on the **Scan Templates** screen to find the Linux compliance scan policy you have created:

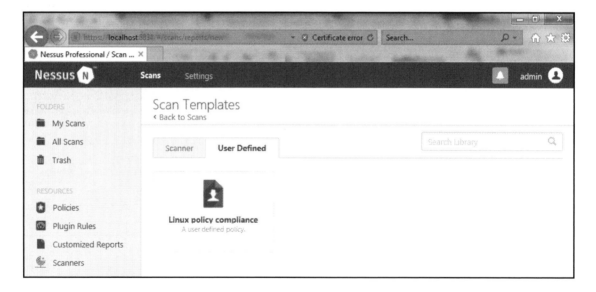

Select the **Policy** and enter the required details, such as the name, description, and target list. To identify the IP address of the test system, run the `ifconfig` command:

```
msfadmin@metasploitable:~$ ifconfig
eth0      Link encap:Ethernet  HWaddr 00:0c:29:74:1c:63
          inet addr:192.168.75.137  Bcast:192.168.75.255  Mask:255.255.255.0
          inet6 addr: fe80::20c:29ff:fe74:1c63/64 Scope:Link
          UP BROADCAST RUNNING MULTICAST  MTU:1500  Metric:1
          RX packets:2786 errors:0 dropped:0 overruns:0 frame:0
          TX packets:172 errors:0 dropped:0 overruns:0 carrier:0
          collisions:0 txqueuelen:1000
          RX bytes:188676 (184.2 KB)  TX bytes:20942 (20.4 KB)
          Interrupt:17 Base address:0x2000

lo        Link encap:Local Loopback
          inet addr:127.0.0.1  Mask:255.0.0.0
          inet6 addr: ::1/128 Scope:Host
          UP LOOPBACK RUNNING  MTU:16436  Metric:1
          RX packets:764 errors:0 dropped:0 overruns:0 frame:0
          TX packets:764 errors:0 dropped:0 overruns:0 carrier:0
          collisions:0 txqueuelen:0
          RX bytes:332277 (324.4 KB)  TX bytes:332277 (324.4 KB)
```

8. Enter the `192.168.75.137` IP address and select **Launch** from the drop-down menu:

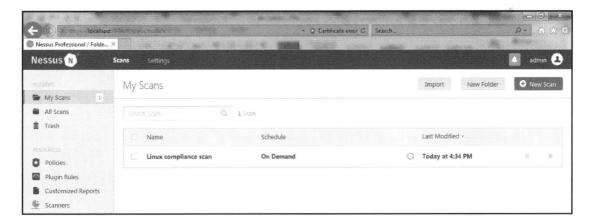

9. Once the scan is completed, open the scan by clicking on it as follows:

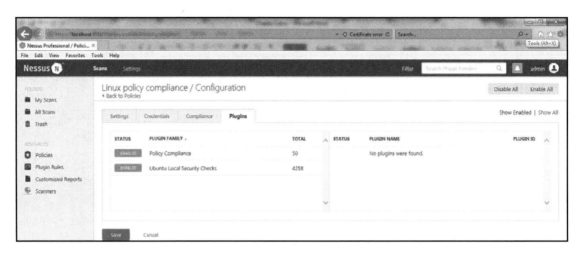

There are four tabs that should appear once you open the results:

- **Hosts**
- **Vulnerabilities**
- **Compliance**
- **History**

These tabs are shown in the following screenshot:

Navigate to the **Vulnerabilities** column. This will display the patches that are missing in the remote Ubuntu host:

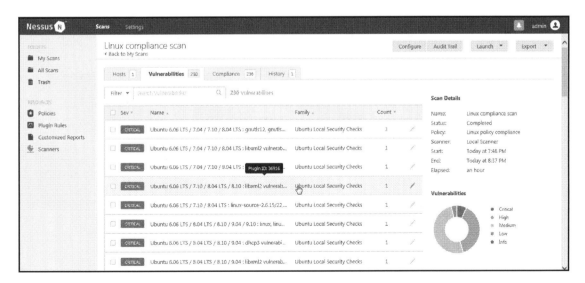

Each vulnerability, as listed by Nessus, consists of the following sections, with additional plugin details to help a user understand the vulnerability better and mitigate by applying the recommended solution:

- **Description**
- **Solution**
- **See also**
- **Output**
- **Port**
- **Host**

Navigate to the **Compliance** tab to check the gaps in the configuration from the CIS benchmark audit file used:

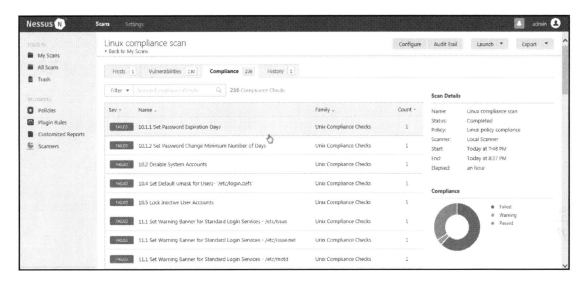

Each compliance consists of the following sections and reference information to help the user understand the gap between the baseline and current configuration:

- **Description**
- **Solution**
- **See also**
- **Output**

- **Audit file**
- **Policy value**
- **Port**
- **Host**

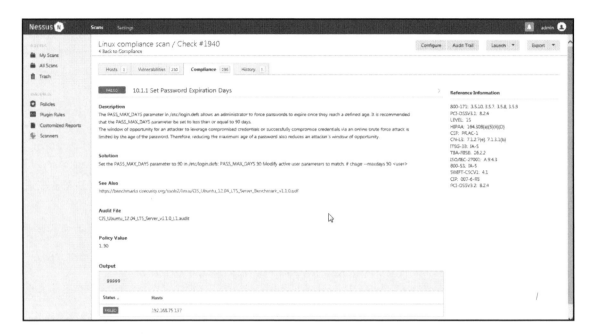

The major difference between the vulnerability scan and the compliance scan is the ratings. Results for the vulnerability scan are reported in terms of their severity: high, medium, low, and informational risk, based on multiple factors including CVSS score and ease of exploitation. By contrast, in a compliance scan, the observations are reported as **failed**, **warning**, and **passed**, where **passed** means the configuration is secure, and **failed** points toward a gap in the configuration.

How it works...

A configuration audit of an operating system allows a user to understand the gaps present in the configuration of the operating system. A simple USB open access can lead to a network takeover these days, given the sophisticated viruses, malware, and adware available on the market. The WannaCry malware in Windows was one such example where an obsolete SMB version allowed the attackers to target millions of machines all over the world. Hence, it is always necessary, as a matter of routine, to include the configuration of the operating system in the audit in order to be fully secure and compliant.

Performing a database audit

In the previous recipes, we have seen a great deal about the need for a configuration audit and its contribution toward more secure networks. In this recipe, we will be looking at using the compliance scan feature of Nessus to perform a configuration audit of a MariaDB database.

Getting ready

The *Getting ready* section for this recipe is same as the *Getting ready* section of the *Selecting a compliance scan policy* section. Further, instead of using the Metasploitable virtual machine as the test setup, we are going to use the Kali Linux operating system. You can download the Kali Linux ISO from `https://www.offensive-security.com/kali-linux-vm-vmware-virtualbox-image-download/`. Download and unzip the package to find a `.vmx` file, as in the *Getting ready* section of *Selecting a compliance scan policy* section.

Use the following syntax to start the MySQL service and set a password for the default user root so that we can remotely log in to the service using the same credentials to perform the audit:

- – `service myql start`: To start the MySQL service
- – `mysql -u root`: To log in using the root user
- – `use mysql`: To select a MySQL table
- – `update user set password=PASSWORD("NEW-ROOT-PASSWORD") where User='root';`: To update the password for the root user in the MySQL table

This should look something like the following:

```
root@kali:~# service mysql start
root@kali:~# mysql -u root
Welcome to the MariaDB monitor.  Commands end with ; or \g.
Your MariaDB connection id is 32
Server version: 10.1.26-MariaDB-1 Debian buildd-unstable

Copyright (c) 2000, 2017, Oracle, MariaDB Corporation Ab and others.

Type 'help;' or '\h' for help. Type '\c' to clear the current input statement.

MariaDB [(none)]> use mysql
Reading table information for completion of table and column names
You can turn off this feature to get a quicker startup with -A

Database changed
MariaDB [mysql]> update user set password=PASSWORD("toor") where User='root';
Query OK, 1 row affected (0.18 sec)
Rows matched: 1  Changed: 1  Warnings: 0

MariaDB [mysql]> Ctrl-C -- exit!
```

How do it...

Perform the following steps:

1. Open the Nessus Web Client.
2. Log in to the Nessus Web Client with the user details created during installation.
3. Click on the **Policies** tab and Select **Create a new policy**.
4. Select **Advanced Scan** and fill in the required details as follows:

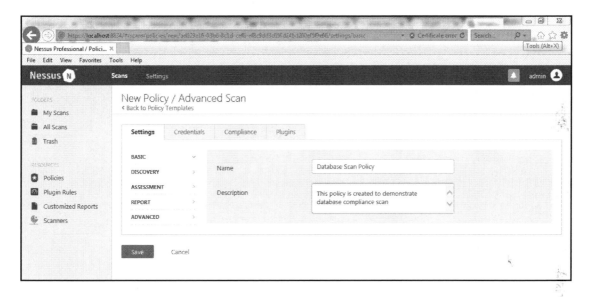

5. Navigate to the **Compliance** tag and search for MySQL benchmarks available in Nessus:

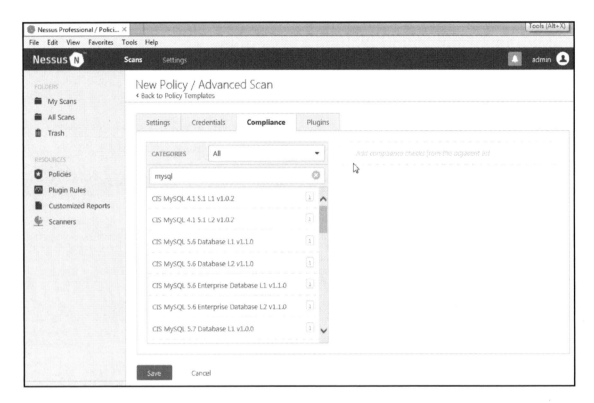

6. The screenshot in the *Getting ready* section shows that the remote host runs MariaDB 10.1.26; thus, we can conclude that the compatible version is MySQL 5.6, as seen at `https://mariadb.com/kb/en/library/mariadb-vs-mysql-compatibility/`.

7. Select **CIS MySQL 5.6 for Linux OS** as a policy to perform a compliance scan:

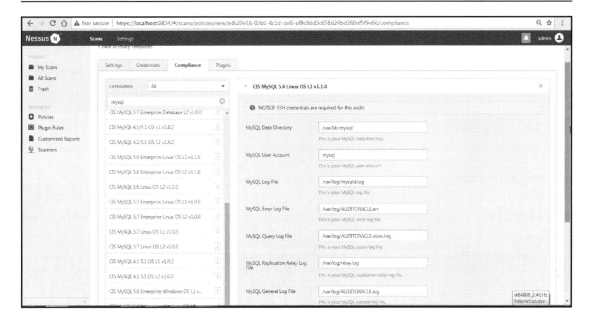

You can change the default paths of the policy if necessary.

8. Navigate to the **Credentials** tab, select **Database** from the drop-down menu, and enter the required details:

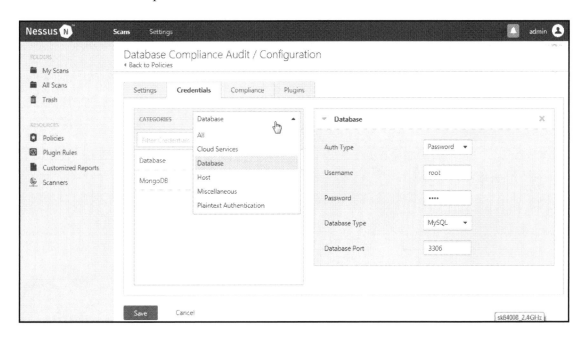

9. Navigate to the **Plugins** tab and disable all the plugins that are not required for the scan:

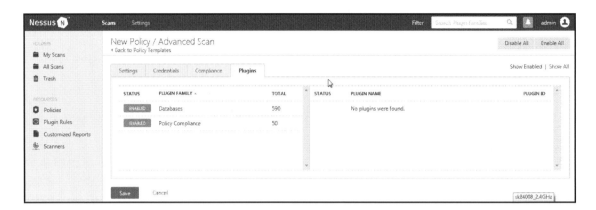

10. Save the policy and navigate to the **Scans** page to create a **New Scan**.

11. Navigate to the **User Defined** policy section to find the policy created for the database compliance scan:

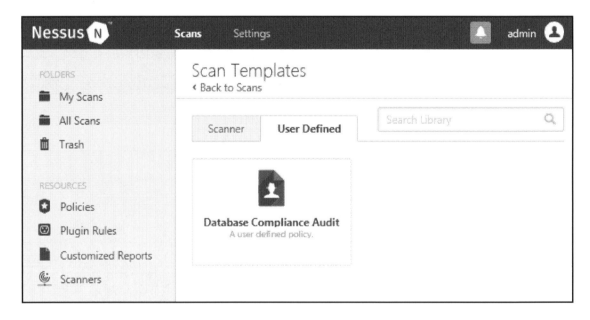

12. Select the **Policy** and fill in the required details, such as the scan name, description, and targets to be scanned:

```
root@kali:~# ifconfig
eth0: flags=4163<UP,BROADCAST,RUNNING,MULTICAST>  mtu 1500
        inet 192.168.75.136  netmask 255.255.255.0  broadcast 192.168.75.255
        inet6 fe80::20c:29ff:fe5a:b29d  prefixlen 64  scopeid 0x20<link>
        ether 00:0c:29:5a:b2:9d  txqueuelen 1000  (Ethernet)
        RX packets 394  bytes 29891 (29.1 KiB)
        RX errors 0  dropped 0  overruns 0  frame 0
        TX packets 99  bytes 8251 (8.0 KiB)
        TX errors 0  dropped 0 overruns 0  carrier 0  collisions 0
        device interrupt 19  base 0x2000

lo: flags=73<UP,LOOPBACK,RUNNING>  mtu 65536
        inet 127.0.0.1  netmask 255.0.0.0
        inet6 ::1  prefixlen 128  scopeid 0x10<host>
        loop  txqueuelen 1000  (Local Loopback)
        RX packets 28  bytes 1596 (1.5 KiB)
        RX errors 0  dropped 0  overruns 0  frame 0
        TX packets 28  bytes 1596 (1.5 KiB)
        TX errors 0  dropped 0 overruns 0  carrier 0  collisions 0
```

The IP address of the remote host can be obtained using the `ifconfig` command. Enter the `192.168.75.136` IP address in the **Targets** field and select **Launch** to begin the scan:

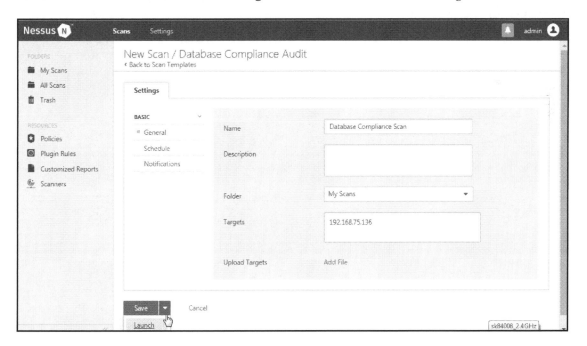

How it works...

A database configuration audit covers a wide spectrum of checks, ranging from logins to schema-level access granted to the user. The previous scan technique helps highlight the missing patches to in the MySQL server and the failed compliance checks.

Performing a web application scan

Nessus also supports web application scans. This can be used to audit and identify vulnerabilities in web applications.

Nessus plugins are effective enough to identify critical vulnerabilities from the OWASP Top 10. Nessus provides options for the user to provide authentication details in order to perform a detailed scan and report various vulnerabilities. As a part of web application tests, Nessus also scans for vulnerabilities in application servers, web servers, and databases; that is, end-to-end vulnerability scanning.

Getting ready

The *Getting ready* section for this recipe is same as the *Getting ready* section of the *Selecting a compliance scan policy* section. This recipe will also require you to have studied and practiced the previous recipes in this chapter. Metasploitable consists of multiple vulnerable applications. In this recipe, we will be using DVWA to demonstrate Nessus' capability to perform web application tests:

The default login credentials for the DVWA application are `admin` for the **Username** field and `password` as the **Password**, as follows:

How do it...

Perform the following steps:

1. Open the Nessus Web Client.
2. Log in to the Nessus Web Client with the user details created during installation.
3. Navigate to the **Policies** page and **Create a new policy** by selecting the web application tests scan template.
4. Fill in the name of the policy and navigate to the credentials:

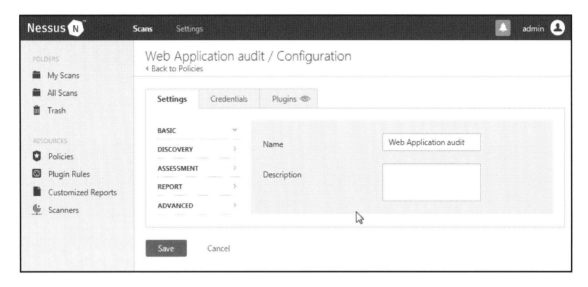

5. Select **HTTP** authentication and fill in the remaining parameters according to the application to be audited:

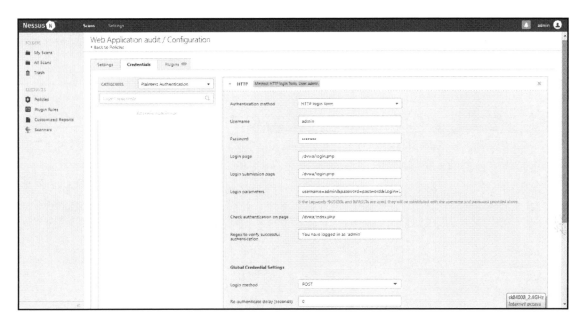

There are multiple parameters to be filled in for this authentication form, such as **Username**, **Password**, path to **Login page**, path to **Login Submission page**, **Login parameters**, path to **Check authentication on page**, and **Regex to verify successful authentication**. Most of these could be obtained by spending a couple of minutes observing the workings of the application and the request it sends to the server from the browser console:

6. Save the policy and navigate to the **Scans** page to create a new scan.

7. Navigate to the **User Define** policies to find the **Web Application audit** policy file:

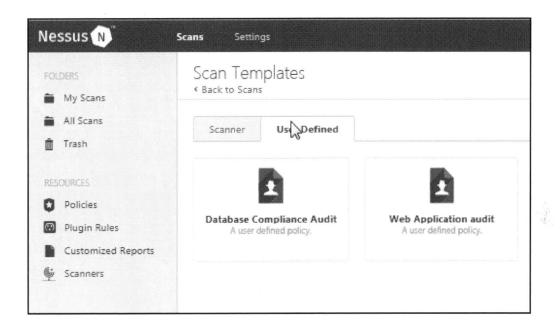

8. Select the appropriate policy and fill in the details such as **Name**, **Description**, and **Targets**. You can simply enter the IP address or the domain name of the host, without any prefix or suffix path:

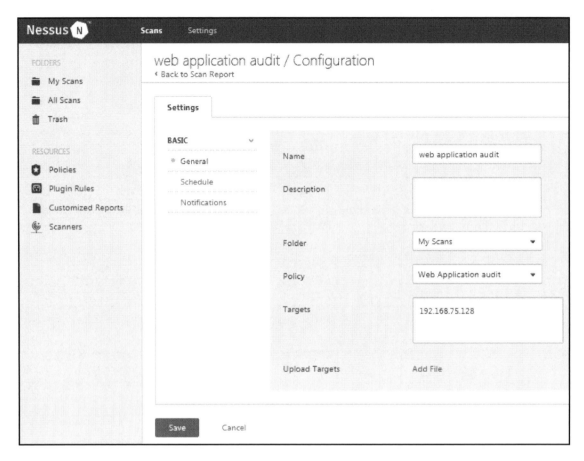

9. Launch the scan and wait for it to complete.
10. Once the scan is complete, open it to see the following info:

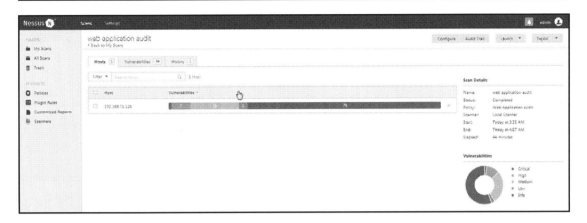

11. Navigate to the **Vulnerabilities** tab to check the reported observations:

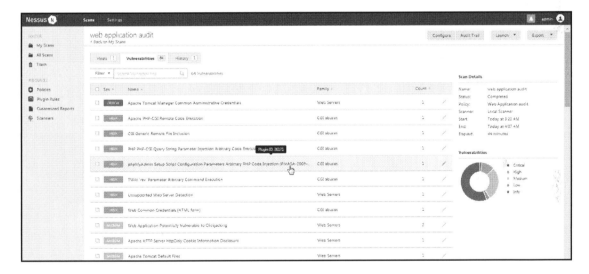

Each vulnerability consists of the following sections, along with other plugin details, to help you understand the vulnerability, as follows:

- **Description**
- **Solution**
- **See also**
- **Output**
- **Port**
- **Hosts**

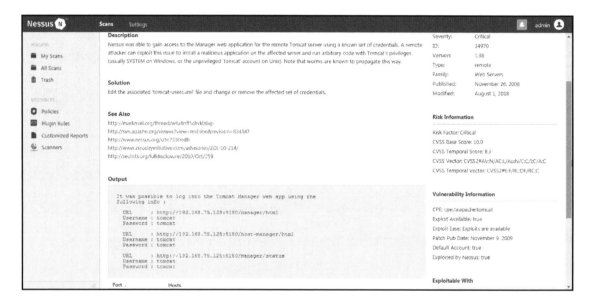

How it works...

The Nessus plugins test the web application against the test cases configured, and report the failed vulnerabilities along with the respective outputs. The report also reveals a great deal about the exploits that were executed by the scanner in order to help the user to recreate the issue and create a better mitigation method. The Nessus web application scanner cannot perform any business logic checks, as it lacks the decision-making algorithms for these. Hence it is always good to use the Nessus web application scanner module only for quick tests and later perform a full fledged penetration test on the application to obtain better results.

6
Report Analysis and Confirmation

In this chapter, we will cover the following recipes:

- Understanding Nmap outputs
- Understanding Nessus outputs
- How to confirm Nessus vulnerabilities using Nmap and other tools

Introduction

In this chapter, we will be going through various recipes regarding the reports that can be generated using Nmap and Nessus. We will also look at a recipe on using Nmap to confirm vulnerabilities that are reported by Nessus. It is always required to confirm the vulnerabilities reported by a scanner, as there are chances of the scanner reporting false positive vulnerabilities. Confirming these vulnerabilities will allow the administrative team to focus on the confirmed vulnerabilities instead of wasting resources on false positives that have been reported. Both Nmap and Nessus generate different formats of reports, allowing the user to make a choice as per their requirements.

Understanding Nmap outputs

Nmap displays results based on the responses it receives from the remote hosts. The more hosts that are scanned, the more complex the results are that are printed on the screen. Analyzing these results when printed in terminal or Command Prompt becomes impossible when the number of hosts increases. In order to solve this problem, Nmap supports various reporting formats which can be used as per the user's requirements. One of the simplest ways to store Nmap's output is to use a >> operator followed by a text file name such as output.txt. This will allow Nmap to forward all the contents to that text file. Even the content of a text file becomes a nightmare to analyze for 10+ hosts. Nmap also gives a lot of verbose and debug information, along with a port scan, which can complicate this process even more. The operating system's detection and fingerprinting adds a lot more junk to this data.

The following command is used to run a SYN scan on the IP address 192.168.75.128 and store the output displayed to the output.txt file. This file can be found in the C:\Users\admin folder since Command Prompt is running in the same folder. Furthermore, you can store this file anywhere by just mentioning the absolute path of the file in double quotes:

```
Nmap –sS –Pn192.168.65.128>> output.txt
```

Let's see how the result can be copied to a text file by going through the following screenshots:

Navigate to the Nmap installation folder and locate the `output.txt` file:

Zotero	14-05-2018 13:53	File folder	
.gitconfig	01-05-2018 09:20	GITCONFIG File	1 KB
_netrc	05-08-2018 12:09	File	1 KB
HKCU_Software.reg	01-05-2018 10:41	Registration Entries	4,731 KB
output.txt	22-09-2018 02:09	Text Document	1 KB

You can open this file using any text editor. I personally recommend Notepad++ as it allows you to perform complex analysis on text files and displays them in a segregated manner:

```
C:\Users\admin\output.txt - Notepad++
File  Edit  Search  View  Encoding  Language  Settings  Tools  Macro  Run  Plugins  Window  ?

output.txt
 1   Starting Nmap 7.70 ( https://nmap.org ) at 2018-09-22 02:08 Arabian Standard Time
 2   Nmap scan report for 192.168.75.128
 3   Host is up (0.0049s latency).
 4   Not shown: 977 closed ports
 5   PORT      STATE SERVICE
 6   21/tcp    open  ftp
 7   22/tcp    open  ssh
 8   23/tcp    open  telnet
 9   25/tcp    open  smtp
10   53/tcp    open  domain
11   80/tcp    open  http
12   111/tcp   open  rpcbind
13   139/tcp   open  netbios-ssn
14   445/tcp   open  microsoft-ds
15   512/tcp   open  exec
16   513/tcp   open  login
17   514/tcp   open  shell
18   1099/tcp  open  rmiregistry
19   1524/tcp  open  ingreslock
20   2049/tcp  open  nfs
21   2121/tcp  open  ccproxy-ftp
22   3306/tcp  open  mysql
23   5432/tcp  open  postgresql
24   5900/tcp  open  vnc
25   6000/tcp  open  X11
26   6667/tcp  open  irc
27   8009/tcp  open  ajp13
28   8180/tcp  open  unknown
29   MAC Address: 00:0C:29:74:1C:63 (VMware)
30
31   Nmap done: 1 IP address (1 host up) scanned in 29.49 seconds
```

Nmap allows a user to define the output format using command-line flags. The following lists explains the different flags that are allowed by Nmap:

- **Interactive output**: This is the type of output that is directly displayed in terminal or Command Prompt. This does not require any special Command Prompt argument or flag as this is the basic and default output format. This result is not stored or saved in any location; one can only access this output as long as Command Prompt or Terminal is not closed.

- **Normal output** (-oN): This output allows the user to save the interact output into a file selected by the user. This reporting option further trims down the output by omitting unnecessary verbose data from the interactive output scan based on the level of verbosity chosen by the user. This will allow the user to have a better look at the port scan results by omitting data that is not required. If a user needs performance data such as scan time and alerts, this is not the right format to choose. Furthermore, you can specify the file folder location by mentioning the absolute path or by launching Command Prompt with the same location as its path.

- **XML output** (-oX): This type of output is required to upload Nmap data to various tools and websites. Once this format is uploaded to any tool, it is then parsed by a parser so that we can understand the various data types in the output and segregate the data accordingly. There are many XML parses available as open source which are custom-built by various tool OEMs.

- **Grepable output** (-oG): This format allows users to perform simple operations such as `grep`, `awk`, `cut`, and `diff` on the output that's generated. The format follows a structure of creating a single-line output for every host with appropriate delimiters so that the user can use simple existing tools in the OS to separate and analyse the results. The Notepad++ utility is one such example that allows delimiter-based separation, which can be used to create a more meaningful report.

- **Script kiddie** (-oS): This format prints the output in the script.

- **Save in all formats** (-oA): This flag allows the user to generate output in the three formats mentioned previously (-oN, -oX, and –oG). Instead of performing three different scans to obtain the output formats, one can simply use this flag to obtain all the three reported formats and save it in a file at a provided location.

Nmap also provides various other details as part of the scan results, some of which can be controlled by the verbosity options that are available. The following are the few extra pieces of data that are produced by the verbose option:

- **Scan completion time estimates**: Nmap also provides performance data such as scan completion time in minutes to seconds, which allows the user to understand the time taken for Nmap to perform the scan. Nmap updates the user between intervals on the time taken and the task being performed, along with the percentage of completion. This allows the user to monitor network scans for larger networks and improve the script's execution time occasionally.
- **Open ports**: In a normal scan without verbose enabled, all of the open ports are displayed at the end of the scans. Instead, if verbose is enabled, each open port is displayed as soon as it is detected.
- **Additional warnings**: Nmap also displays any warnings or errors that have occurred during the scan, whether the port scan is taking additional time, or any variance from normal behavior of the scan. This will allow the user to check for any network restrictions and act accordingly.
- **OS detection information**: OS detection in Nmap is performed using signature detection based on TCP ISN and IP ID prediction. If verbose is enabled and the OS detection option is selected, Nmap displays the prediction of these OSes.
- **Host status**: Nmap also prints the status of the host as detected during runtime, stating whether the host is live or dead:

```
C:\Windows\system32\cmd.exe

C:\Users\admin>nmap -sS -Pn 192.168.75.128 -v
Starting Nmap 7.70 ( https://nmap.org ) at 2018-09-22 02:48 Arabian Standard Time
Initiating ARP Ping Scan at 02:48
Scanning 192.168.75.128 [1 port]
Completed ARP Ping Scan at 02:48, 1.67s elapsed (1 total hosts)
Initiating Parallel DNS resolution of 1 host. at 02:49
Completed Parallel DNS resolution of 1 host. at 02:49, 16.50s elapsed
Initiating SYN Stealth Scan at 02:49
Scanning 192.168.75.128 [1000 ports]
Discovered open port 23/tcp on 192.168.75.128
Discovered open port 5900/tcp on 192.168.75.128
Discovered open port 22/tcp on 192.168.75.128
Discovered open port 445/tcp on 192.168.75.128
Discovered open port 139/tcp on 192.168.75.128
Discovered open port 111/tcp on 192.168.75.128
Discovered open port 80/tcp on 192.168.75.128
Discovered open port 25/tcp on 192.168.75.128
Discovered open port 6000/tcp on 192.168.75.128
Discovered open port 1524/tcp on 192.168.75.128
Discovered open port 8009/tcp on 192.168.75.128
Discovered open port 2121/tcp on 192.168.75.128
Discovered open port 512/tcp on 192.168.75.128
Discovered open port 2049/tcp on 192.168.75.128
Discovered open port 5432/tcp on 192.168.75.128
Discovered open port 1099/tcp on 192.168.75.128
Discovered open port 8180/tcp on 192.168.75.128
Discovered open port 514/tcp on 192.168.75.128
Discovered open port 6667/tcp on 192.168.75.128
Discovered open port 513/tcp on 192.168.75.128
Discovered open port 53/tcp on 192.168.75.128
Discovered open port 21/tcp on 192.168.75.128
Discovered open port 3306/tcp on 192.168.75.128
Completed SYN Stealth Scan at 02:49, 1.11s elapsed (1000 total ports)
Nmap scan report for 192.168.75.128
Host is up (0.0018s latency).
```

Some of the options that can be used along with the verbose ones to control the data displayed in the output are as follows:

- **Debug output**: Debug mode is an additional flag option provided by Nmap to help the user with further data to understand the port scanning process at the packet level. This can be enabled by appending the verbosity syntax with –d. Furthermore, you can also set the debug level you want to enable, which ranges up to 9, by appending –d9 to the verbose syntax. This is the highest level of debugging and provides a lot of technical data about the port scan being performed:

- **Packet trace**: This option allows the user to obtain the track of each packet that Nmap is sending. This will allow the user to gain a detailed understanding of the scan. This can be configured by appending --packet-trace to the verbose syntax:

Getting ready

In order to complete this activity, you will have to satisfy the following prerequisites on your machine:

1. You must have Nmap installed.
2. You must have network access to the hosts on which the scans are to be performed.

In order to install Nmap, you can follow the instructions provided in Chapter 2, *Understanding Network Scanning Tools*. This will allow you to download a compatible version of Nmap and install all the required plugins. In order to check whether your machine has Nmap installed, open Command Prompt and type Nmap. If Nmap is installed, you will see a screen similar to the following:

```
C:\Windows\system32\cmd.exe

Microsoft Windows [Version 6.1.7601]
Copyright (c) 2009 Microsoft Corporation.  All rights reserved.

C:\Users\admin>nmap
Nmap 7.70 ( https://nmap.org )
Usage: nmap [Scan Type(s)] [Options] {target specification}
TARGET SPECIFICATION:
  Can pass hostnames, IP addresses, networks, etc.
  Ex: scanme.nmap.org, microsoft.com/24, 192.168.0.1; 10.0.0-255.1-254
  -iL <inputfilename>: Input from list of hosts/networks
  -iR <num hosts>: Choose random targets
  --exclude <host1[,host2][,host3],...>: Exclude hosts/networks
  --excludefile <exclude_file>: Exclude list from file
HOST DISCOVERY:
  -sL: List Scan - simply list targets to scan
  -sn: Ping Scan - disable port scan
  -Pn: Treat all hosts as online -- skip host discovery
  -PS/PA/PU/PY[portlist]: TCP SYN/ACK, UDP or SCTP discovery to given ports
  -PE/PP/PM: ICMP echo, timestamp, and netmask request discovery probes
  -PO[protocol list]: IP Protocol Ping
  -n/-R: Never do DNS resolution/Always resolve [default: sometimes]
  --dns-servers <serv1[,serv2],...>: Specify custom DNS servers
  --system-dns: Use OS's DNS resolver
  --traceroute: Trace hop path to each host
SCAN TECHNIQUES:
  -sS/sT/sA/sW/sM: TCP SYN/Connect()/ACK/Window/Maimon scans
  -sU: UDP Scan
  -sN/sF/sX: TCP Null, FIN, and Xmas scans
  --scanflags <flags>: Customize TCP scan flags
```

If you do not see the preceding screen, retry the same step by moving the Command Prompt control into the folder where Nmap is installed (`C:\Program Files\Nmap`). If you do not see the screen after doing this, remove and reinstall Nmap.

To populate the open ports on hosts where the scan is going to be performed, you are required to have network-level access to that host. A simple way to check whether you have access to the host is through ICMP by sending ping packets to the host. But this method only works if ICMP and ping are enabled in that network. In cases where ICMP is disabled, live host detection techniques vary. We will look at this in further sections of this book.

In order to obtain the preceding output, we need to install a virtual machine. In order to run a virtual machine, I would recommend using VMware's 30-day trial version, which can be downloaded and installed from `https://www.vmware.com/products/workstation-pro/workstation-pro-evaluation.html`.

For the test system, readers can download Metasploitable (a vulnerable virtual machine by Rapid 7) from `https://information.rapid7.com/download-metasploitable-2017.html`. Perform the following steps to open Metasploitable. This provides various components such as the operating system, database, and a vulnerable application, which will help us test the recipes in this chapter:

1. Unzip the downloaded Metasploitable package:

Metasploitable.nvram	04-09-2018 16:53	NVRAM File		9 KB
Metasploitable.vmdk	17-09-2018 13:48	VMware virtual dis...	18,81,024 KB	
Metasploitable.vmsd	07-05-2010 14:46	VMSD File		0 KB
Metasploitable.vmx	17-09-2018 13:47	VMware virtual m...		3 KB
Metasploitable.vmxf	07-05-2010 14:46	VMXF File		1 KB

2. Open the `.vmx` file using the installed VMware Workstation or VMware Player:

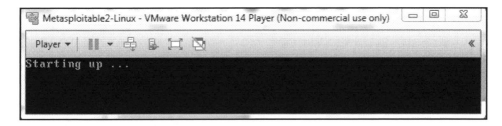

3. Log in using `msfadmin`/`msfadmin` as the username and password:

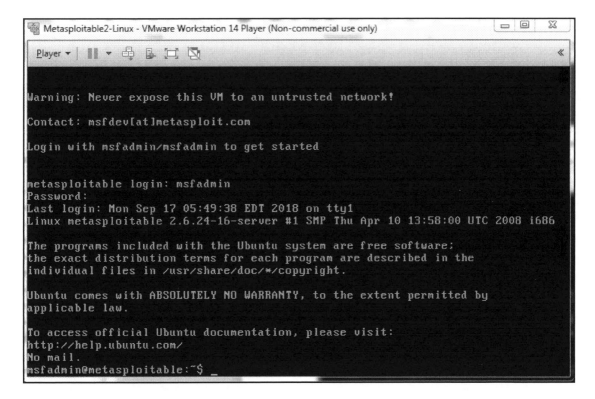

How do it...

Perform the following steps:

1. Open Nmap in Command Prompt.
2. Enter the following syntax in Command Prompt to obtain the interactive output:

   `Nmap -sS -Pn 192.168.103.129`

```
C:\WINDOWS\system32\cmd.exe

C:\>nmap -sS -Pn 192.168.103.129
Starting Nmap 7.70 ( https://nmap.org ) at 2018-09-22 03:52 Arabian Standard Time
Nmap scan report for 192.168.103.129
Host is up (0.0027s latency).
Not shown: 977 closed ports
PORT     STATE SERVICE
21/tcp   open  ftp
22/tcp   open  ssh
23/tcp   open  telnet
25/tcp   open  smtp
53/tcp   open  domain
80/tcp   open  http
111/tcp  open  rpcbind
139/tcp  open  netbios-ssn
445/tcp  open  microsoft-ds
512/tcp  open  exec
513/tcp  open  login
514/tcp  open  shell
1099/tcp open  rmiregistry
1524/tcp open  ingreslock
2049/tcp open  nfs
2121/tcp open  ccproxy-ftp
3306/tcp open  mysql
5432/tcp open  postgresql
5900/tcp open  vnc
6000/tcp open  X11
6667/tcp open  irc
8009/tcp open  ajp13
8180/tcp open  unknown
MAC Address: 00:0C:29:02:9E:B0 (VMware)

Nmap done: 1 IP address (1 host up) scanned in 7.81 seconds
```

3. Enter the following syntax in Command Prompt to obtain the normal output:

```
Nmap -sS -Pn 192.168.103.129 -oN output
```

```
Administrator: Command Prompt

C:\WINDOWS\system32>nmap -sS -Pn 192.168.103.129 -oN output
Starting Nmap 7.70 ( https://nmap.org ) at 2018-09-22 03:57 Arabian Standard Time
Nmap scan report for 192.168.103.129
Host is up (0.0024s latency).
Not shown: 977 closed ports
PORT      STATE SERVICE
21/tcp    open  ftp
22/tcp    open  ssh
23/tcp    open  telnet
25/tcp    open  smtp
53/tcp    open  domain
80/tcp    open  http
111/tcp   open  rpcbind
139/tcp   open  netbios-ssn
445/tcp   open  microsoft-ds
512/tcp   open  exec
513/tcp   open  login
514/tcp   open  shell
1099/tcp  open  rmiregistry
1524/tcp  open  ingreslock
2049/tcp  open  nfs
2121/tcp  open  ccproxy-ftp
3306/tcp  open  mysql
5432/tcp  open  postgresql
5900/tcp  open  vnc
6000/tcp  open  X11
6667/tcp  open  irc
8009/tcp  open  ajp13
8180/tcp  open  unknown
MAC Address: 00:0C:29:02:9E:B0 (VMware)

Nmap done: 1 IP address (1 host up) scanned in 5.95 seconds
```

You can navigate to the `system32` folder to locate the output file and open it with text editing tools:

```
C:\Windows\System32\output - Notepad++
File  Edit  Search  View  Encoding  Language  Settings  Tools  Macro  Run  Plugins  Window  ?

output

  1  # Nmap 7.70 scan initiated Sat Sep 22 03:57:23 2018 as: nmap -sS -Pn -oN output 192.168.103.129
  2  Nmap scan report for 192.168.103.129
  3  Host is up (0.0024s latency).
  4  Not shown: 977 closed ports
  5  PORT       STATE  SERVICE
  6  21/tcp     open   ftp
  7  22/tcp     open   ssh
  8  23/tcp     open   telnet
  9  25/tcp     open   smtp
 10  53/tcp     open   domain
 11  80/tcp     open   http
 12  111/tcp    open   rpcbind
 13  139/tcp    open   netbios-ssn
 14  445/tcp    open   microsoft-ds
 15  512/tcp    open   exec
 16  513/tcp    open   login
 17  514/tcp    open   shell
 18  1099/tcp   open   rmiregistry
 19  1524/tcp   open   ingreslock
 20  2049/tcp   open   nfs
 21  2121/tcp   open   ccproxy-ftp
 22  3306/tcp   open   mysql
 23  5432/tcp   open   postgresql
 24  5900/tcp   open   vnc
 25  6000/tcp   open   X11
 26  6667/tcp   open   irc
 27  8009/tcp   open   ajp13
 28  8180/tcp   open   unknown
 29  MAC Address: 00:0C:29:02:9E:B0 (VMware)
 30
 31  # Nmap done at Sat Sep 22 03:57:28 2018 -- 1 IP address (1 host up) scanned in 5.95 seconds
 32
```

4. Enter the following syntax in Command Prompt to obtain the XML output:

```
Nmap -sS -Pn 192.168.103.129 -oX  output
```

```
C:\WINDOWS\system32>nmap -sS -Pn 192.168.103.129 -oX output
Starting Nmap 7.70 ( https://nmap.org ) at 2018-09-22 04:02 Arabian Standard Time
Nmap scan report for 192.168.103.129
Host is up (0.0033s latency).
Not shown: 977 closed ports
PORT      STATE SERVICE
21/tcp    open  ftp
22/tcp    open  ssh
23/tcp    open  telnet
25/tcp    open  smtp
53/tcp    open  domain
80/tcp    open  http
111/tcp   open  rpcbind
139/tcp   open  netbios-ssn
445/tcp   open  microsoft-ds
512/tcp   open  exec
513/tcp   open  login
514/tcp   open  shell
1099/tcp open  rmiregistry
1524/tcp open  ingreslock
2049/tcp open  nfs
2121/tcp open  ccproxy-ftp
3306/tcp open  mysql
5432/tcp open  postgresql
5900/tcp open  vnc
6000/tcp open  X11
6667/tcp open  irc
8009/tcp open  ajp13
8180/tcp open  unknown
MAC Address: 00:0C:29:02:9E:B0 (VMware)

Nmap done: 1 IP address (1 host up) scanned in 5.49 seconds

C:\WINDOWS\system32>
```

You can navigate to the `system32` folder to locate the output file and open it with text editing tools:

5. Enter the following syntax in Command Prompt to obtain the script kiddie output:

```
Nmap -sS -Pn 192.168.103.129 -oS  output
```

```
C:\WINDOWS\system32>nmap -sS -Pn 192.168.103.129 -oS output
Starting Nmap 7.70 ( https://nmap.org ) at 2018-09-22 04:06 Arabian Standard Time
Nmap scan report for 192.168.103.129
Host is up (0.0027s latency).
Not shown: 977 closed ports
PORT      STATE SERVICE
21/tcp    open  ftp
22/tcp    open  ssh
23/tcp    open  telnet
25/tcp    open  smtp
53/tcp    open  domain
80/tcp    open  http
111/tcp   open  rpcbind
139/tcp   open  netbios-ssn
445/tcp   open  microsoft-ds
512/tcp   open  exec
513/tcp   open  login
514/tcp   open  shell
1099/tcp open  rmiregistry
1524/tcp open  ingreslock
2049/tcp open  nfs
2121/tcp open  ccproxy-ftp
3306/tcp open  mysql
5432/tcp open  postgresql
5900/tcp open  vnc
6000/tcp open  X11
6667/tcp open  irc
8009/tcp open  ajp13
8180/tcp open  unknown
MAC Address: 00:0C:29:02:9E:B0 (VMware)

Nmap done: 1 IP address (1 host up) scanned in 4.71 seconds

C:\WINDOWS\system32>
```

You can navigate to the `system32` folder to locate the output file and open it with text editing tools:

```
C:\Windows\System32\output - Notepad++

File  Edit  Search  View  Encoding  Language  Settings  Tools  Macro  Run  Plugins  Window  ?

output

1   staRtinG nmap 7.70 ( hTtpS://nmap.0rg ) aT 2018-09-22 04:06 ArabIan $tandard TimE
2   nmap scAn rEp0rt f0r 192.168.103.129
3   hO$t Iz up (0.0027z lat3ncy).
4   NOt shOWn: 977 cl0s3d pOrtS
5   POrT      $T4T3 $3RVIC3
6   21/tcp    Op3n  ftP
7   22/tcp    0pen  S$h
8   23/tcp    0PEn  T3lN3t
9   25/tCp    Op3n  $mtp
10  53/tcp    Open  domaIn
11  80/Tcp    op3n  HttP
12  111/tcp   oP3n  rpcb1Nd
13  139/tcp   0p3n  nEtbIoz-$sn
14  445/tcp   op3n  m1CR0S0FT-ds
15  512/tcp   0p3n  3Xec
16  513/tcp   open  L0gin
17  514/Tcp   oPen  Shell
18  1099/tCp  open  rM1R3g!stry
19  1524/tcp  open  InGr3$L0ck
20  2049/tcp  op3n  nfs
21  2121/tcp  op3n  Ccpr0xy-fTp
22  3306/tcp  0pen  mysql
23  5432/Tcp  0peN  p0$tgr3$Ql
24  5900/tCp  0pEn  vnc
25  6000/tcp  0peN  X11
26  6667/tcp  op3n  iRc
27  8009/tcP  0p3n  ajP13
28  8180/Tcp  open  UNkNown
29  M4C 4Ddr3$S: 00:0C:29:02:93:b0 (VMwar3)
30
31  Nmap d0N3: 1 |P addRe$s (1 Ho$t UP) scanNed in 4.71 sEcONdz
32
```

6. Enter the following syntax in Command Prompt to obtain the output in grepable format:

```
Nmap -sS -Pn 192.168.103.129 -v -oG output
```

You can navigate to the `Windows` folder to locate the output file and open it with text editing tools:

7. Enter the following syntax in Command Prompt to obtain the output in all the formats with verbose enabled:

```
Nmap -sS -Pn 192.168.103.129 -v-oA  output
```

```
C:\Windows>nmap -sS -Pn -v 192.168.103.129 -oA output
Starting Nmap 7.70 ( https://nmap.org ) at 2018-09-22 04:15 Arabian Standard Time
Initiating ARP Ping Scan at 04:15
Scanning 192.168.103.129 [1 port]
Completed ARP Ping Scan at 04:15, 0.98s elapsed (1 total hosts)
Initiating Parallel DNS resolution of 1 host. at 04:15
Completed Parallel DNS resolution of 1 host. at 04:15, 0.01s elapsed
Initiating SYN Stealth Scan at 04:15
Scanning 192.168.103.129 [1000 ports]
Discovered open port 139/tcp on 192.168.103.129
Discovered open port 445/tcp on 192.168.103.129
Discovered open port 5900/tcp on 192.168.103.129
Discovered open port 22/tcp on 192.168.103.129
Discovered open port 21/tcp on 192.168.103.129
Discovered open port 3306/tcp on 192.168.103.129
Discovered open port 80/tcp on 192.168.103.129
Discovered open port 23/tcp on 192.168.103.129
Discovered open port 111/tcp on 192.168.103.129
Discovered open port 25/tcp on 192.168.103.129
Discovered open port 53/tcp on 192.168.103.129
Discovered open port 513/tcp on 192.168.103.129
Discovered open port 1099/tcp on 192.168.103.129
Discovered open port 1524/tcp on 192.168.103.129
Discovered open port 2121/tcp on 192.168.103.129
Discovered open port 6667/tcp on 192.168.103.129
Discovered open port 8180/tcp on 192.168.103.129
Discovered open port 512/tcp on 192.168.103.129
Discovered open port 2049/tcp on 192.168.103.129
Discovered open port 514/tcp on 192.168.103.129
Discovered open port 8009/tcp on 192.168.103.129
Discovered open port 5432/tcp on 192.168.103.129
Discovered open port 6000/tcp on 192.168.103.129
Completed SYN Stealth Scan at 04:15, 0.14s elapsed (1000 total ports)
Nmap scan report for 192.168.103.129
Host is up (0.0026s latency).
Not shown: 977 closed ports
PORT    STATE SERVICE
21/tcp  open  ftp
```

You can navigate to the `Windows` folder to locate the output file and open it with text editing tools:

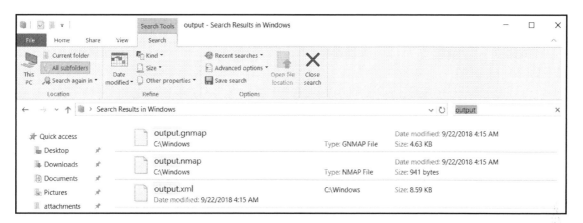

How it works...

These different formats help the user to utilize the reports for multiple operations and analyse the reports in different ways. The port scan results represent a critical phase of reconnaissance, which allows the users to further plan the vulnerability scan and detection activities. These reports are then uploaded to different tools and sites for further analysis and scanning. It is also worth mentioning that Nmap is a background utility for various vulnerability scanning software. Once these reports are generated, these tools use the same to perform further actions.

Understanding Nessus outputs

Nessus is more of an enterprise-aligned tool. The reporting is more comprehensive and user-friendly. Nessus provides document and structure-based reporting. These reports can be exported by selecting the format required in the **Export** drop-down in the top-right corner of the **Scans** result page:

Here, we will go over the reporting formats that are supported by Nessus.

Nessus

This format allows the user to import the results in `.nessus` format. This is a format that can only be parsed using Nessus. It allows users to download the scan results and later import the same into Nessus for any type of analysis to be performed.

HTML

Nessus provides a good illustration of the scan reports in a HTML file format which is standalone and can be opened in any browser to view the results. This report also allows for the navigation between different sections so that users can easily read huge reports. These HTML reports can also be customized to download the following reports:

- Executive Summary report:

- Custom report with vulnerabilities and remediations grouped by host
- Custom report with vulnerabilities and remediations grouped by plugin

A HTML report contains the following sections:

- **TABLE OF CONTENTS**: This lists the required navigation pane for vulnerabilities by host and recommendations. These contain further details in complex reports such as compliance audit:

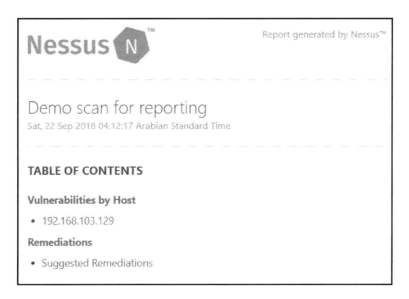

- **Vulnerabilities by host**: This section consists of the actual vulnerabilities by host. This follows the format of reporting all of the vulnerabilities per host and then moving on to the next host. This further starts with a simple summary of the number of vulnerabilities and their risk ratings per host. This includes **Scan Information** such as **Start time** and **End time**, along with **Host Information**:

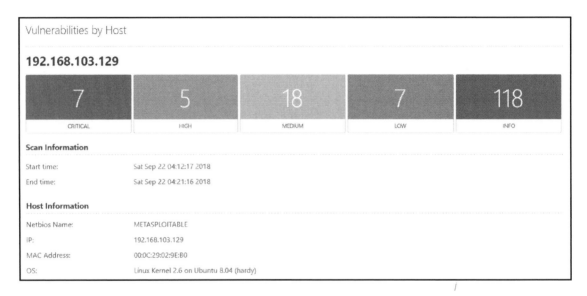

Each vulnerability consists of the following sections, the details of which have been described in Chapter 5, *Configuration Audits*:

- Plugin ID
- Synopsis
- Description
- Solution
- Risk factor
- References

- Plugin information and output:

Vulnerabilities

10114 - ICMP Timestamp Request Remote Date Disclosure

Synopsis

It is possible to determine the exact time set on the remote host.

Description

The remote host answers to an ICMP timestamp request. This allows an attacker to know the date that is set on the targeted machine, which may assist an unauthenticated, remote attacker in defeating time-based authentication protocols.

Timestamps returned from machines running Windows Vista / 7 / 2008 / 2008 R2 are deliberately incorrect, but usually within 1000 seconds of the actual system time.

Solution

Filter out the ICMP timestamp requests (13), and the outgoing ICMP timestamp replies (14).

Risk Factor

None

References

CVE   CVE-1999-0524
XREF   CWE:200

Plugin Information:

Published: 1999/08/01, Modified: 2018/08/10

Plugin Output

icmp/0

```
The difference between the local and remote clocks is -2 seconds.
```

CSV

CSV is a simple format used to store data in tables, which can later be imported to databases and applications such as Excel. This allows the user to export the report into a `.csv` file, which can be opened using tools such as Excel. The following is a screenshot of a sample CSV report:

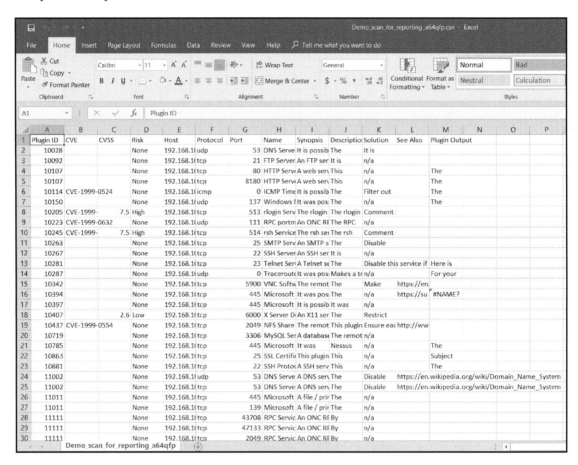

It holds similar sections to the ones mentioned for the HTML format.

Nessus DB

This is a custom database-like format proprietary to Nessus. It is an encrypted format that's used to store the scan's details:

It requires a password to be created and used every time it is imported into Nessus.

Getting ready

In order to perform this activity, you will have to satisfy the following prerequisites on your machine:

1. You must have Nessus installed.
2. You must have network access to the hosts on which the scans are to be performed.

In order to install Nesus, you can follow the instructions provided in Chapter 2, *Understanding Network Scanning Tools*. This will allow you to download a compatible version of Nessus and install all the required plugins. To check whether your machine has Nessus installed, open the search bar and search for Nessus Web Client. Once found and clicked, this will be opened in the default browser window:

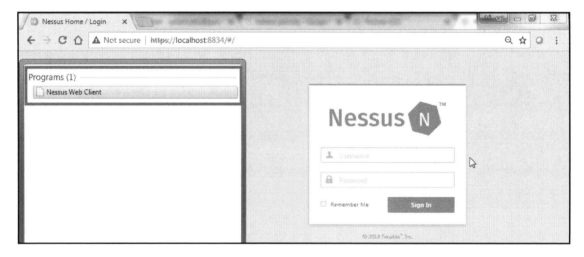

If you are sure that Nessus has been installed correctly, you can use the `https://localhost:8834` URL directly from your browser to open the Nessus Web Client. If you are unable to locate the **Nessus Web Client**, you should remove and reinstall Nessus. For the removal of Nessus and installation instructions, refer to `Chapter 2`, *Understanding Network Scanning Tools*. If you have located the **Nessus Web Client** and are unable to open it in the browser window, you need to check whether the Nessus service is running in the Windows Services utility:

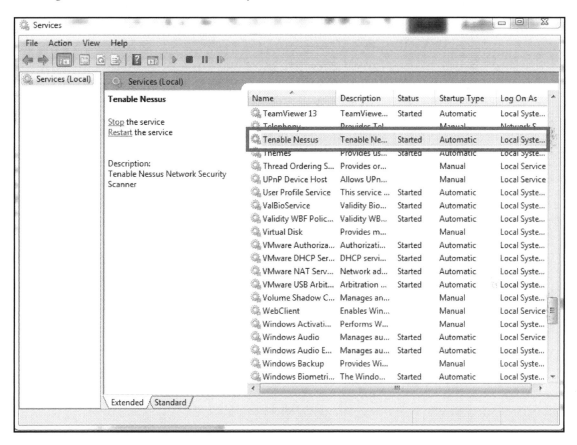

You can further start and stop Nessus by using the Services utility as per your requirements. In order to further confirm the installation using the command-line interface, you can navigate to the installation directory to see and access Nessus' command-line utilities:

```
C:\Windows\system32\cmd.exe

C:\>cd "Program Files"

C:\Program Files>cd Tenable

C:\Program Files\Tenable>cd Nessus

C:\Program Files\Tenable\Nessus>dir
 Volume in drive C has no label.
 Volume Serial Number is B234-0E80

 Directory of C:\Program Files\Tenable\Nessus

16-07-2018  11:45    <DIR>          .
16-07-2018  11:45    <DIR>          ..
16-07-2018  11:45                 1 .winperms
19-06-2018  17:25            45,113 License.rtf
19-06-2018  19:25         6,459,904 nasl.exe
19-06-2018  19:25            46,592 ndbg.exe
19-06-2018  17:25                46 Nessus Web Client.url
19-06-2018  19:22            17,424 nessus-service.exe
19-06-2018  19:25         6,405,120 nessuscli.exe
19-06-2018  19:25         6,837,776 nessusd.exe
               8 File(s)     19,811,976 bytes
               2 Dir(s)   1,970,270,208 bytes free

C:\Program Files\Tenable\Nessus>
```

It is always recommended to have administrator-level or root-level credentials to provide the scanner with access to all the system files. This will allow the scanner to perform a deeper scan and populate better results compared to a non-credentialed scan, as without proper privileges, the system will not have access to all the files and folders. The policy compliance module is only available in the paid versions of Nessus, such as Nessus Professional or Nessus Manager. For this, you will have to purchase an activation key from tenable and update it in the settings page, as shown in the following screenshot:

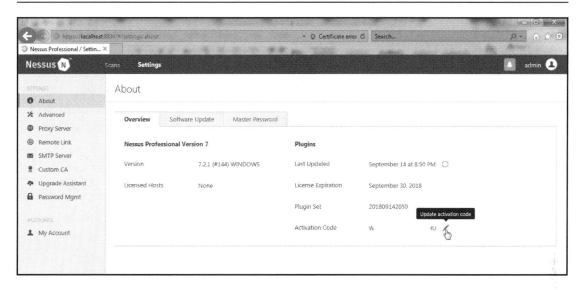

Click on the edit button to open a window and enter a new activation code, which you will have purchased from tenable:

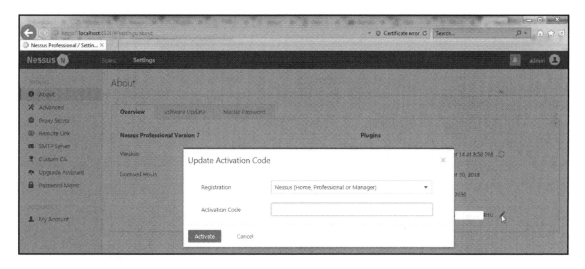

In order to test the scans, we need to install a virtual machine. In order to run a virtual machine, I would recommend using VMware's 30-day trial version, which can be downloaded and installed from `https://www.vmware.com/products/workstation-pro/workstation-pro-evaluation.html`.

For the test system, readers can download Metasploitable by referring to the *Getting ready* section of the previous recipe.

How do it...

Perform the following steps:

1. Open the Nessus web client.
2. Log in to the Nessus client with the user that you created during installation.
3. Perform a simple network scan on the virtual machine and open the scan results:

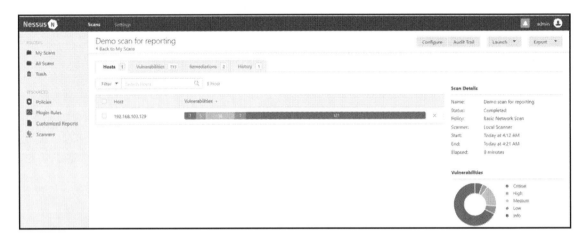

4. Navigate to the export functionality and select the Nessus format to download the `.nessus` version of the report:

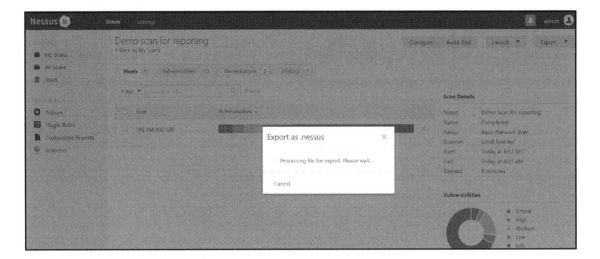

5. Navigate to the export functionality and select the Nessus format to download the HTML version of the report by selecting the required options:

6. Navigate to the export functionality and select the Nessus format to download the CSV version of the report:

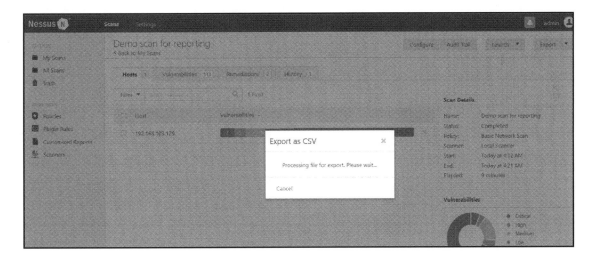

7. Navigate to the export functionality and select the Nessus format to download the Nessus DB version of the report:

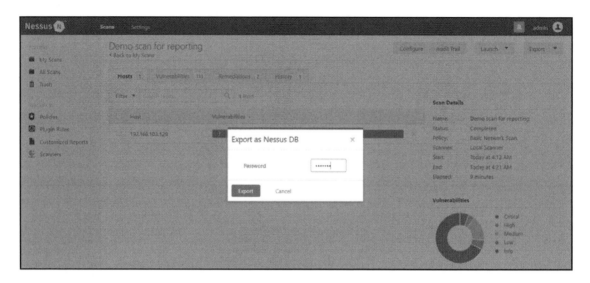

Enter a desired password and click on **Export** to download the Nessus DB file with the extension `.db`.

How it works...

The supported report formats by Nessus allow a user to present the report in multiple ways. If the user wants to store the scan results in a secure manner, they can use the DB format, which is encrypted. If the user wants to share the report directly, they can use the HTML format of the report. For further analysis, they can use the CSV format to import the report results into tools or software. If the user requires to share scan results with other administrators, they can use the .nessus format, where the administrator can import the file into their own Nessus and perform further analysis.

> For a CSV report, if there are multiple CSV reports and a user requires to merge all the reports in Windows, they can open Command Prompt from the folder where all the CSV files are located and use the copy *.csv <name of the new file>.csv command, thereby obtaining a merged CSV single file. Further filtering and removal of duplicates with sorting allows you to create a linear report.

How to confirm Nessus vulnerabilities using Nmap and other tools

Most of the vulnerabilities reported by Nessus are signature and value-based, which Nessus makes a decision on based on the code present in the plugins. It is required to confirm these vulnerabilities using manual techniques such as Nmap scripts or port-specific open source tools. This will allow the administration team to put their efforts into the mitigation of the actual vulnerabilities instead of false positives. Also, sometimes, Nessus reports vulnerabilities for which workarounds have already been applied as Nessus only checks with respect to the conditions mentioned in the plugin and cannot recognize any other deviations. In this recipe, we will look at sets to verify multiple vulnerabilities reported by Nessus using Nmap and other open source tools.

In order to create this recipe, we will perform a demo basic network scan on Metasploitable 2's vulnerable virtual machine (look at the *Getting ready* section in order to download this). Once the scan is complete, a glance at the results will display a total of seven critical, five high, 18 medium, and seven low vulnerabilities. Out of the vulnerabilities reported by Nessus, we will try to manually confirm the following vulnerabilities:

- **Bind shell backdoor detection**: This is a critical-risk vulnerability that's reported by Nessus. This vulnerability points out that a port on the remote host is allowing any user on the network to run a shell with root privileges on the vulnerable virtual machine. We will use the Windows Telnet utility to confirm this vulnerability:

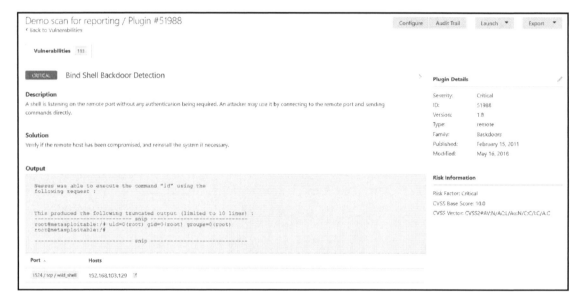

- **SSL version 2 and 3 protocol detection**: This is a high-risk vulnerability that's reported by Nessus. This vulnerability pertains to the usage of a legacy SSL protocol, such as SSL version 2 and version 3, which are known to cause multiple vulnerabilities. We will use Nmap script to confirm this vulnerability:

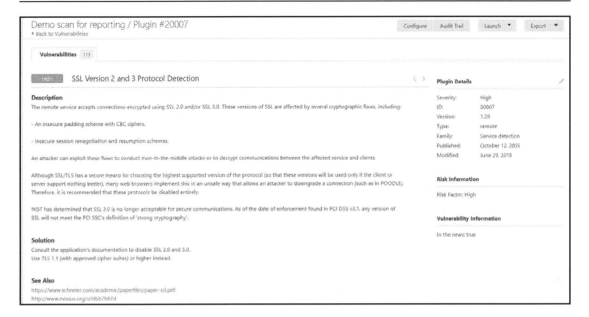

- **Apache Tomcat default files**: This is a medium-risk vulnerability that's reported by Nessus. This vulnerability mentions various default files which are created upon the installation of Apache tools. These are still available for any user on the network without authentication. We will use a web browser (Chrome, in this case) to confirm this vulnerability.

Getting ready

In order to create a setup for this, you need to follow and perform all the steps mentioned in the *Getting ready* section of the previous recipes, *Understanding Nmap outputs* and *Understanding Nessus outputs*.

How do it...

Perform the following steps:

1. To confirm bind shell backdoor detection, open Command Prompt in Windows and type the following command:

   ```
   telnet 192.168.103.129 1524
   ```

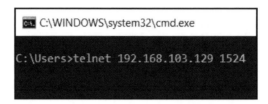

2. Upon execution, the user directly gets logged in to the remote machine without providing any authentication:

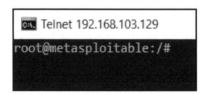

3. To confirm the privilege of the user, we will use the standard Linux command `id` to confirm the vulnerability:

```
Telnet 192.168.103.129
root@metasploitable:/# id
uid=0(root) gid=0(root) groups=0(root)
                                        root@metasploitable:/# root@metasploitable:/#
```

This command displays the UID and GID as 0, which represents a root user, and so we can confirm that the vulnerability is critical as it allows any remote user to log in to the machine without any authentication. This means that the vulnerability can be confirmed.

4. For SSL v2 and SSL v3, we can identify the version running by using the Poodle confirmation script by Nmap, as only SSL v3 is vulnerable to Poodle. Open Nmap in Command Prompt.

5. Enter the following command to identify whether the remote server is vulnerable to an SSL Poodle attack:

```
Nmap -sV -script ssl-poodle -p 25 192.168.103.129
```

```
C:\Windows>nmap -sV -script ssl-poodle -p 25 192.168.103.129
Starting Nmap 7.70 ( https://nmap.org ) at 2018-09-22 07:27 Arabian Standard Time
Nmap scan report for 192.168.103.129
Host is up (0.00s latency).

PORT     STATE SERVICE VERSION
25/tcp open  smtp      Postfix smtpd
MAC Address: 00:0C:29:02:9E:B0 (VMware)
Service Info: Host:  metasploitable.localdomain

Service detection performed. Please report any incorrect results at https://nmap.org/submit/ .
Nmap done: 1 IP address (1 host up) scanned in 61.36 seconds
```

As Nmap has not displayed any results, let's check for the `ssl-enum-ciphers` script:

```
C:\Windows>nmap -script=ssl-enum-ciphers -p 25 192.168.103.129
Starting Nmap 7.70 ( https://nmap.org ) at 2018-09-22 07:33 Arabian Standard Time
Nmap scan report for 192.168.103.129
Host is up (0.00013s latency).

PORT     STATE SERVICE
25/tcp open  smtp
MAC Address: 00:0C:29:02:9E:B0 (VMware)

Nmap done: 1 IP address (1 host up) scanned in 50.98 seconds

C:\Windows>
```

Even the `enum-ciphers` script has not returned any result, so we can conclude that Nmap was unable to negotiate with the port using SSL ciphers. Hence, we can mark the vulnerability as a false positive. We can also confirm the same by using Telnet on port 25 if a similar response is received. This means that port 25 is running on a non-SSL clear text protocol and the plugin has reported a false positive for the same:

```
Telnet 192.168.103.129
       220 metasploitable.localdomain ESMTP Postfix (Ubuntu)
EHLO
502 5.5.2 Error: command not recognized
HELO
501 Syntax: HELO hostname
HELO example.com
250 metasploitable.localdomain
help
502 5.5.2 Error: command not recognized
```

6. To confirm the Apache default files, access the URLs mentioned by Nessus in the vulnerability output section:

Output

```
The following default files were found :

/tomcat-docs/index.html
/nessus-check/default-404-error-page.html
```

Port ▲	Hosts
8180 / tcp / www	192.168.103.129

---

7. Open the browser and type
   `http://192.168.103.129:8180/tomcat-docs/index.html` into the address bar:

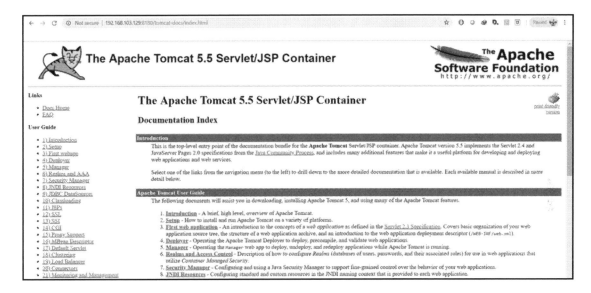

This displays the default documentation folder, confirming the existence of the default files on the server. This shows that the vulnerability can be confirmed.

How it works...

These vulnerabilities can be identified based on their risk and then confirmed, allowing the analyst to prioritize their efforts on the vulnerability they are trying to confirm. Identifying these false positives requires effort as you have to actually exploit the vulnerability and check whether it is feasible. In order to do this, an analyst must decide to what extent they are willing to expend effort in order to fix the vulnerability. For example, if the vulnerability is that port `1406` with a SQL service running is open to everyone in the network, it is up to the analyst to decide whether to just check for the open port or try logging in to the SQL service using a default service account or a weak password.

7
Understanding the Customization and Optimization of Nessus and Nmap

In this chapter, we will cover the following recipes:

- Understanding the Nmap Script Engine and its customization
- Understanding the Nessus Audit policy and its customization

Introduction

It is clear now from the previous chapters that Nmap Script Engine and Nessus' Compliance Audit policy are an important part of both tools to perform comprehensive audits and checks. It is very important for a user to understand the workings of these components and the various techniques to customize them in order to perform specific operations. In this chapter, we will look at the details of Nmap Script Engine and Nessus Audit file compositions in order to create custom files and perform specific operations.

Understanding Nmap Script Engine and its customization

The Nmap Script Engine is used to run custom scripts written by users to automate network-level actions. Typically, Nmap scripts end with a `.nse` extension. These scripts are used to perform the following tasks:

- **Host and port discovery**: The whole purpose of Nmap being so widely used is to perform simple tasks to check whether the remote host is live or non-live, along with the current status of the ports.
- **Version detection**: Nmap has a database of a variety of application and service signatures which are checked against the responses received from the ports to identify the service running on the port and sometimes the specific version as well.
- **Affected vulnerabilities**: Nmap Script Engine allows users to determine whether a particular port/service is vulnerable to a specific disclosed vulnerability. It depends on the script written by the user to query data from the service running and sends custom packets based on a response to determine whether the port/service is actually vulnerable. The Nmap scripts use the Lua programming language, and we will be looking into a few syntax as a part of this recipe to write a custom script. All the Nmap scripts are categorized into the following categories:
  - `auth`: This category of script deals with any authentication-related check, for example, default username and password logins, and anonymous and null logins.
  - `broadcast`: This category of script is used to add newly discovered hosts dynamically which are to be scanned by Nmap, allowing the user to perform a full network discovery and scan at the same time.
  - `brute`: This category of the script is used to perform a brute force attack to guess the password for various services such as HTTP, database, FTP, and so on.
  - `default`: This category of script is run along with all the scans where specific scripts are not mentioned in the command line.

- `discovery`: This category of script is used to obtain further information about network services on their shared resources within the network .
- `dos`: This category of script would be one of the most unwanted in the Nmap scripts. These scripts are used to test vulnerabilities which cause **Denial of Service (DoS)** attacks by crashing the service.
- `exploit`: These scripts are used to exploit specific vulnerabilities.
- `external`: This category of script uses external resources to perform the given task. For example, for any DNS-related scripts, Nmap will have to query the local DNS servers.
- `fuzzer`: This category of script is used to generate random payloads to exploit a specific service. The response of the service to these payloads can be used to determine whether a particular service is vulnerable.
- `intrusive`: This category of script is used to directly exploit the vulnerability. These scans must be used in a later phase after reconnaissance.
- `malware`: This category of script allows the user to identify if the remote host is affected by any malware or has any backdoor open.
- `safe`: This category of script is used to grab data which is available to everyone in the network such as banners, keys, and so on.
- `version`: This category of script is used to identify and determine the versions of the services running on the remote host.
- `vuln`: This category of script is used to verify specific vulnerabilities.

Syntax

The following are the arguments which are required in an `nmap` command in order to execute the script:

- `--script <filename>|<category>|<directory>|<expression>`: This argument allows the user to specify the script to be executed, where the filename, category, directory, and expression follow in order to help the user select the scripts. In order for the user to execute these scripts, they need to be present in the scripts folder of the Nmap installation directory:

Name	Date modified	Type	Size
acarsd-info.nse	17-03-2018 06:40	NSE File	4 KB
address-info.nse	17-03-2018 06:40	NSE File	9 KB
afp-brute.nse	17-03-2018 06:40	NSE File	4 KB
afp-ls.nse	17-03-2018 06:40	NSE File	7 KB
afp-path-vuln.nse	17-03-2018 06:40	NSE File	7 KB
afp-serverinfo.nse	17-03-2018 06:40	NSE File	6 KB
afp-showmount.nse	17-03-2018 06:40	NSE File	3 KB
ajp-auth.nse	17-03-2018 06:40	NSE File	3 KB
ajp-brute.nse	17-03-2018 06:40	NSE File	3 KB
ajp-headers.nse	17-03-2018 06:40	NSE File	2 KB
ajp-methods.nse	17-03-2018 06:40	NSE File	3 KB
ajp-request.nse	17-03-2018 06:40	NSE File	3 KB
allseeingeye-info.nse	17-03-2018 06:40	NSE File	7 KB
amqp-info.nse	17-03-2018 06:40	NSE File	2 KB
asn-query.nse	17-03-2018 06:40	NSE File	15 KB
auth-owners.nse	17-03-2018 06:40	NSE File	3 KB
auth-spoof.nse	17-03-2018 06:40	NSE File	1 KB
backorifice-brute.nse	17-03-2018 06:40	NSE File	10 KB
backorifice-info.nse	17-03-2018 06:40	NSE File	10 KB
bacnet-info.nse	17-03-2018 06:40	NSE File	41 KB
banner.nse	17-03-2018 06:40	NSE File	6 KB
bitcoin-getaddr.nse	17-03-2018 06:40	NSE File	2 KB
bitcoin-info.nse	17-03-2018 06:40	NSE File	2 KB
bitcoinrpc-info.nse	17-03-2018 06:40	NSE File	5 KB
bittorrent-discovery.nse	17-03-2018 06:40	NSE File	4 KB
bjnp-discover.nse	17-03-2018 06:40	NSE File	2 KB

The generic syntax used here is as follows:

```
nmap  --script afp-ls.nse <host>
```

- `--script-args`: This allows the user to pass inputs to the `nmap` command if required. The generic syntax used here is as follows:

```
nmap  --script afp-ls.nse --script-args <arguments> <host>
```

- `--script-args-file`: This allows the user to upload file inputs to the `nmap` command. The generic syntax used here is as follows:

```
nmap  --script afp-ls.nse --script-args-file <filename/path> <host>
```

- `--script-help <filename>|<category>|<directory>|<expression>`: This argument will allow the user to obtain more information about the scripts which can be used. The generic syntax used here is as follows:

```
nmap  --script-help <filename>
```

```
C:\Windows\system32\cmd.exe

C:\Users\admin>nmap --script-help smb* >> D:/output.txt
C:\Users\admin>_
```

As the output was huge, we saved it to a file called `output.txt` in the D drive. Open the `output` file in a text editor to see the help message:

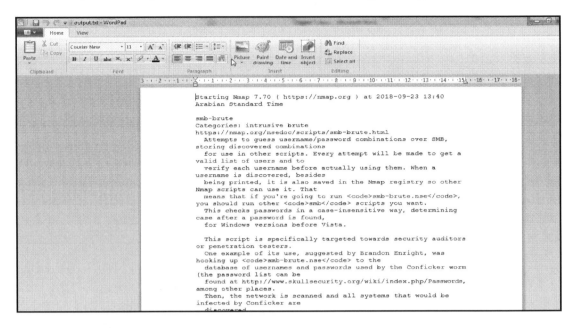

- `--script-trace`: If used, this argument will allow the user to view the network communication being performed by the script:

    ```
    nmap --script afp-ls.nse –script-trace <hostname>
    ```

- `--script-updatedb`: This is used to update the script's database, which is used by Nmap. The generic syntax used here is as follows:

    ```
    nmap --script-updatedb
    ```

Environment variables

The following are the environment variables used in preparing an Nmap script:

- `SCRIPT_PATH`: This describes the path of the script
- `SCRIPT_NAME`: This describes the name given to the script
- `SCRIPT_TYPE`: This variable is used to describe the type of rule which has invoked by the script for a remote host

The following is a structure of a simple Nmap script:

```
//Rule section
portrule = function(host, port)
    return port.protocol == "tcp"
            and port.number == 25
            and port.state == "open"
end

//Action section
action = function(host, port)
    return "smtp port is open"
end
```

Script template

An Nmap script is basically categorized into three sections, which are discussed here. We will use the script from `https://svn.nmap.org/nmap/scripts/smtp-enum-users.nse` as an example to define the data in these categories:

- `Head`: This section holds the descriptive and dependency related data to the script, the below are the various supported components:
    - `description`: This field acts as metadata to the script and describes important information about the script's function in order for the user to make use of it. It attempts to enumerate the users on a SMTP server by issuing the `VRFY`, `EXPN`, or `RCPT TO` commands. The goal of this script is to discover all of the user accounts in the remote system. The script will output the list of usernames that were found. The script will stop querying the SMTP server if authentication is enforced. If an error occurs while testing the target host, the error will be printed with the list of any combinations that were found prior to the error. The user can specify which methods to use and in which order. The script will ignore repeated methods. If not specified, the script will use `RCPT` first, then `VRFY` and `EXPN`. An example of how to specify the methods to use and the order is shown as follows:

```
description = [[
<code>smtp-enum-users.methods={EXPN,RCPT,VRFY}</code>
]]
```

- `Categories`: This field allows the user to map the nature of the script by mentioning the category it belongs to. As seen in the preceding introduction, we can mention the categories by using the following syntax from the `smtp-enum-users.nse` script:

```
categories = {"auth","external","intrusive"}
```

- `author`: This field allows the author of the script to provide information about themselves such as their name, contact information, website, email, and so on:

```
author = "Duarte Silva <duarte.silva@serializing.me>"
```

- `license`: This field is used to mention any license details required to distribute the script, along with the standard Nmap installation:

```
license = "Same as Nmap--See
https://nmap.org/book/man-legal.html"
```

- `dependencies`: This field defines the run level of the script, which means if any script is dependent on the output from any other script, the same can be mentioned here, allowing the dependent script to be executed first. This output can then be passed to script two:

```
dependencies = {"dependant script"}
```

- **Script libraries**: Nmap Script Engine uses variables to allow different scripts to be built upon a similar service. By using dependencies from libraries, authors can write comprehensive and small scripts. The following table explains some of the scan libraries:

Ajp	cassandra
Amqp	citrixxml
asn1	Comm
base32	Creds
base64	Cvs
Bin	Datafiles
Bit	Dhcp
Bitcoin	dhcp6

Bittorrent	Dns
Bjnp	Dnsbl
Brute	Dnssd
Eigrp	Drda
ftp	Eap

For reference, we can look at the script at `https://svn.nmap.org/nmap/scripts/` `smtp-enum-users.nse` to see how the libraries are defined:

```
local nmap = require "nmap"
local shortport = require "shortport"
local smtp = require "smtp"
local stdnse = require "stdnse"
local string = require "string"
local table = require "table"
local unpwdb = require "unpwdb"
```

These libraries have various functions defined in them, for which we can pass arguments using the following syntax: `<function name>(arg1, arg2, arg3)`. For example, `smtp.check_reply("MAIL", response)`.

- `Rules`: The script rules are used to determine whether a remote host is to be scanned or not based on the Boolean outcome of true or false. The host is only scanned when the rule returns true. Here are the rules which are applied on the host by a script:
  - `prerule()`: This rule is executed before the scan is performed on the hosts
  - `hostrule(host)`, `portrule(host, port)`: These rules are executed after each set of hosts have been scanned using the provided script
  - `postrule()`: This rule is executed once all the host scans are completed

The following is the rule used in the example script `smtp-enum-users.nse`:

```
portrule = shortport.port_or_service({ 25, 465, 587 },
  { "smtp", "smtps", "submission" })
```

- `Action`: This section consists of the actions to be performed by the script. Once the action is executed, it returns a specific result based on which the end result seen by the user is determined. The following is the action section from the example script `smtp-enum-users.nse`:

```
action = function(host, port)
  local status, result = go(host, port)
  -- The go function returned true, lets check if it
  -- didn't found any accounts.
  if status and #result == 0 then
    return stdnse.format_output(true, "Couldn't find any accounts")
  end
```

Some of the libraries require the script to be in specific formats and must use the NSEDoc format. We will see how to fit the script into such a format in this recipe. In this recipe, we will have a look at creating a script to identify whether default Tomcat files are present on a remote host.

Getting ready

In order to complete this activity, you will have to satisfy the following prerequisites on your machine:

- You must have Nmap installed.
- You must have network access to the hosts on which the scans are to be performed.

In order to install Nmap, you can follow the instructions provided in Chapter 2, *Understanding Network Scanning Tools*. This will allow you to download a compatible version of Nmap and install all the required plugins. In order to check whether your machine has Nmap installed, open the Command Prompt and type nmap. If Nmap is installed, you will see a screen similar to the following:

```
C:\Windows\system32\cmd.exe

Microsoft Windows [Version 6.1.7601]
Copyright (c) 2009 Microsoft Corporation.  All rights reserved.

C:\Users\admin>nmap
Nmap 7.70 ( https://nmap.org )
Usage: nmap [Scan Type(s)] [Options] {target specification}
TARGET SPECIFICATION:
  Can pass hostnames, IP addresses, networks, etc.
  Ex: scanme.nmap.org, microsoft.com/24, 192.168.0.1; 10.0.0-255.1-254
  -iL <inputfilename>: Input from list of hosts/networks
  -iR <num hosts>: Choose random targets
  --exclude <host1[,host2][,host3],...>: Exclude hosts/networks
  --excludefile <exclude_file>: Exclude list from file
HOST DISCOVERY:
  -sL: List Scan - simply list targets to scan
  -sn: Ping Scan - disable port scan
  -Pn: Treat all hosts as online -- skip host discovery
  -PS/PA/PU/PY[portlist]: TCP SYN/ACK, UDP or SCTP discovery to given ports
  -PE/PP/PM: ICMP echo, timestamp, and netmask request discovery probes
  -PO[protocol list]: IP Protocol Ping
  -n/-R: Never do DNS resolution/Always resolve [default: sometimes]
  --dns-servers <serv1[,serv2],...>: Specify custom DNS servers
  --system-dns: Use OS's DNS resolver
  --traceroute: Trace hop path to each host
SCAN TECHNIQUES:
  -sS/sT/sA/sW/sM: TCP SYN/Connect()/ACK/Window/Maimon scans
  -sU: UDP Scan
  -sN/sF/sX: TCP Null, FIN, and Xmas scans
  --scanflags <flags>: Customize TCP scan flags
```

If you do not see the preceding screen, retry the same steps by moving the Command Prompt control into the folder where Nmap is installed (C:\Program Files\Nmap). If you do not see the preceding screen after this, remove and reinstall Nmap.

To populate the open ports on hosts for which the scan is to be done, you are required to have network-level access to that particular host. A simple way to check whether you have access to the particular host is through ICMP by sending ping packets to the host. However, this method only works if ICMP and ping are enabled in that network. If ICMP is disabled, live host detection techniques vary. We will look at this in more detail in later sections of this book.

In order to obtain the output shown, you are required to install a virtual machine. To be able to run a virtual machine, I would recommend using VMware's 30-day trial version, which can be downloaded and installed from https://www.vmware.com/products/workstation-pro/workstation-pro-evaluation.html.

For the test system, readers can download Metasploitable (a vulnerable virtual machine by Rapid 7) from https://information.rapid7.com/download-metasploitable-2017.html. Follow these steps to open Metasploitable. This provides various components like the operating system, database, and vulnerable applications, which will help us test the recipes in this chapter. Follow these instructions to get started:

1. Unzip the downloaded Metasploitable package
2. Open the .vxm file using the installed VMware Workstation or VMware Player
3. Log in using msfadmin/msfadmin as the username and password

How do it...

Perform the following steps:

1. Open a text editor and define three sections, Head, Rule, and Action, as shown in the following screenshot:

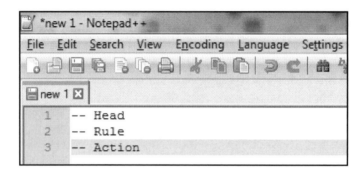

2. Let's start with the Head section. The following are the parameters which are to be mentioned in the Head section with the following code:

```
-- Head
description = [[Sample script to check whether default apache files
are present]]
author = "Jetty"
license = "Same as Nmap--See http://nmap.org/book/man-legal.html"
categories = {"default", "safe"}
-- Rule
-- Action
```

3. Now, let's define the libraries required for the script to function by using the following code:

```
local shortport = require "shortport"
local http = require "http"
```

In order for the script to write port rules, we need to use `shortport` and `http`. We use `shortport` to generate the port rule and `http` to simplify communication with HTTP and HTTPS pages.

4. Let's now start with the rule section by introducing the `shortport` rule from the `shortport` library that's included. This allows Nmap to invoke actions if the port is open:

```
portrule = shortport.http
```

5. Once the `Head` and `Rule` section are completed, all we have to do is define the `action` page to perform the decisive operation and determine whether the default Tomcat documents exist at the location mentioned in the URI:

```
action = function(host, port)
    local uri = "/tomcat-docs/index.html"
    local response = http.get(host, port, uri)
    if ( response.status == 200 ) then
        return response.body
    end
end
```

In the action section, we are defining the URI which needs to be checked for default files. We are fetching the response using the `http.get` function and saving it in the variable response. Then, we have laid an if condition to check whether the HTTP response received from the server consists of HTTP code 200, which depicts that the page was fetched successfully. Now, to actually see the contents of the web page, we are printing the response received using `response.body`.

6. Let's try and execute the script we have written for now to check whether it is working or needs troubleshooting. The following is a screenshot of the script. Save it to the Nmap installation directory in the scripts folder with the name `apache-default-files.nse`:

```
C:\Program Files (x86)\Nmap\scripts\apache-default-files.nse - Notepad++ [Administrator]
File  Edit  Search  View  Encoding  Language  Settings  Tools  Macro  Run  Plugins  Window  ?

apache-default-files.nse

 1   -- Head
 2
 3   description = [[Sample script to check whether default apache files are present]]
 4   author = "Jetty"
 5   license = "Same as Nmap--See http://nmap.org/book/man-legal.html"
 6   categories = {"default", "safe"}
 7
 8   local shortport = require "shortport"
 9   local http = require "http"
10
11   -- Rule
12   portrule = shortport.http
13
14   -- Action
15   action = function(host, port)
16       local uri = "/tomcat-docs/index.html"
17       local response = http.get(host, port, uri)
18       if ( response.status == 200 ) then
19           return response.body
20       end
21   end
22
```

Execute the script by using the following syntax:

```
nmap --script apache-default-files 192.168.75.128 -p8180 -v
```

```
C:\Users\admin>nmap --script apache-default-files 192.168.75.128 -p8180 -v
Starting Nmap 7.70 ( https://nmap.org ) at 2018-09-23 15:54 Arabian Standard Time
NSE: Loaded 1 scripts for scanning.
NSE: Script Pre-scanning.
Initiating NSE at 15:54
Completed NSE at 15:54, 0.00s elapsed
Initiating ARP Ping Scan at 15:54
Scanning 192.168.75.128 [1 port]
Completed ARP Ping Scan at 15:54, 1.70s elapsed (1 total hosts)
Initiating Parallel DNS resolution of 1 host. at 15:54
Completed Parallel DNS resolution of 1 host. at 15:54, 16.50s elapsed
Initiating SYN Stealth Scan at 15:54
Scanning 192.168.75.128 [1 port]
Discovered open port 8180/tcp on 192.168.75.128
Completed SYN Stealth Scan at 15:54, 0.01s elapsed (1 total ports)
NSE: Script scanning 192.168.75.128.
Initiating NSE at 15:54
Completed NSE at 15:54, 0.02s elapsed
Nmap scan report for 192.168.75.128
Host is up (0.00s latency).

PORT     STATE SERVICE
8180/tcp open  unknown
| apache-default-files: <html><head><META http-equiv="Content-Type" content="text/html; charset=iso-8859-1"><title>The Apache Tomcat 5.5 Servlet/JSP Container - Documen
</title><meta value="Craig R. McClanahan" name="author"><meta value="craigmcc@apache.org" name="email"><meta value="Remy Maucherat" name="author"><meta value="remm@apac
="email"><meta value="Yoav Shapira" name="author"><meta value="yoavs@apache.org" name="email"></head><body vlink="#525D76" alink="#525D76" link="#525D76" text="#000000"
fffff"><table cellspacing="0" width="100%" border="0"><!--PAGE HEADER--><tr><td><!--PROJECT LOGO--><a href="http://tomcat.apache.org/"><img border="0" alt="
|     The Apache Tomcat Servlet/JSP Container
|      " align="right" src="./images/tomcat.gif"/></a></td><td><font face="arial,helvetica,sanserif"><h1>The Apache Tomcat 5.5 Servlet/JSP Container</h1></font></td><td><
GO--><a href="http://www.apache.org/"><img border="0" alt="Apache Logo" align="right" src="./images/asf-logo.gif"/></a></td></tr></table><table cellspacing="4" width="10
0"><!--HEADER SEPARATOR--><tr><td colspan="2"><hr size="1" noshade></td></tr><tr><!--LEFT SIDE NAVIGATION--><td nowrap="true" valign="top" width="20%"><p><strong>Links</
<ul><li><a href="index.html">Docs Home</a></li></ul><p><strong>User Guide</strong></p><ul><li><a href="introducti
Introduction</a></li><li><a href="setup.html">2) Setup</a></li><li><a href="appdev/index.html">3) First webapp</a></li><li><a href="deployer-howto.html">4) Deployer</a>
href="manager-howto.html">5) Manager</a></li><li><a href="realm-howto.html">6) Realms and AAA</a></li><li><a href="security-manager-howto.html">7) Security Manager</a>
ref="jndi-resources-howto.html">8) JNDI Resources</a></li><li><a href="jndi-datasource-examples-howto.html">9) JDBC DataSources</a></li><li><a href="class-loader-howto.
assloading</a></li><li><a href="jasper-howto.html">11) JSPs</a></li><li><a href="ssl-howto.html">12) SSL</a></li><li><a href="ssi-howto.html">13) SSI</a></li><li><a href
.html">14) CGI</a></li><li><a href="proxy-howto.html">15) Proxy Support</a></li><li><a href="mbeans-descriptor-howto.html">16) MBean Descriptor</a></li><li><a href="def
.html">17) Default Servlet</a></li><li><a href="cluster-howto.html">18) Clustering</a></li><li><a href="balancer-howto.html">19) Load Balancer</a></li><li><a href="conn
>20) Connectors</a></li><li><a href="monitoring.html">21) Monitoring and Management</a></li><li><a href="logging.html">22) Logging</a></li><li><a href="apr.html">23) AP
><a href="virtual-hosting-howto.html">24) Virtual Hosting</a></li></ul><p><strong>Reference</strong></p><ul><li><a href="RELEASE-NOTES.txt">Release Notes</a></li><li><
ig/index.html">Apache Tomcat Configuration</a></li><li><a href="http://tomcat.apache.org/connectors-doc/">JK 1.2 Documentation</a></li><li><a href="servletapi/index.htm
PI Javadocs</a></li><li><a href="jspapi/index.html">JSP API Javadocs</a></li></ul><p><strong>Apache Tomcat Development</strong></p><ul><li><a href="building.html">Build
<li><a href="changelog.html">Changelog</a></li><li><a href="status.html">Status</a></li><li><a href="developers.html">Developers</a></li><li><a href="catalina-funcspecs
>Functional Specs.</a></li><li><a href="catalina/docs/api/index.html">Apache Tomcat Javadocs</a></li><li><a href="jasper/docs/api/index.html">Apache Jasper Javadocs</a>
href="architecture/index.html">Architecture</a></li></ul></td><!--RIGHT SIDE MAIN BODY--><td align="left" valign="top" width="80%"><table cellspacing="4" width="100%" b
r><td valign="top" align="left"><h1>The Apache Tomcat 5.5 Servlet/JSP Container</h1><h2>Documentation Index</h2></td><td nowrap="true" valign="top" align="right"><small
inter/index.html"><img alt="Printer Friendly Version" border="0" src="./images/printer.gif"><br>print-friendly<br>version
|          </a></small></td></tr></table><table cellpadding="2" cellspacing="0" border="0"><tr><td bgcolor="#525D76"><font face="arial,helvetica,sanserif" co
"><a name="Introduction"><strong>Introduction</strong></a></font></td></tr><tr><td><blockquote>
```

The preceding screenshot shows that the script has been executed successfully and the page retrieved is the default page of Apache Tomcat. This means that the host is vulnerable. Now, instead of printing such heavy outputs, we can change the value of the return variable to vulnerable.

It is not always concluded that a 200 response means that the remote host is vulnerable, as the response might contain a custom error message. Therefore, it is recommended to include regex-based conditions to conclude the same and then return the response accordingly.

7. Let's further decorate the script in the format and write script documentation for it by adding the following lines to the script in the `Head` section:

```
---
-- @usage
-- nmap --script apache-default-files` <target>
-- @output
-- PORT    STATE SERVICE
-- |_apache-default-files: Vulnerable
```

The script now looks something like this:

```
-- Head
description = [[Sample script to check whether default apache files
are present]]
author = "Jetty"
license = "Same as Nmap--See http://nmap.org/book/man-legal.html"
categories = {"default", "safe"}


---
-- @usage
-- nmap --script apache-default-files` <target>
-- @output
-- PORT    STATE SERVICE
-- |_apache-default-files: Vulnerable


local shortport = require "shortport"
local http = require "http"


-- Rule
portrule = shortport.http


-- Action
action = function(host, port)
    local uri = "/tomcat-docs/index.html"
    local response = http.get(host, port, uri)
    if ( response.status == 200 ) then
        return "vulnerable"
    end
end
```

8. Save the script in the `scripts` folder of the Nmap installation directory and execute it using the following syntax:

   nmap --script apache-default-files 192.168.75.128 –p8180 –v

```
C:\Users\admin>nmap --script apache-default-files 192.168.75.128 -p8180 -v
Starting Nmap 7.70 ( https://nmap.org ) at 2018-09-23 16:07 Arabian Standard Time
NSE: Loaded 1 scripts for scanning.
NSE: Script Pre-scanning.
Initiating NSE at 16:07
Completed NSE at 16:07, 0.00s elapsed
Initiating ARP Ping Scan at 16:07
Scanning 192.168.75.128 [1 port]
Completed ARP Ping Scan at 16:07, 1.77s elapsed (1 total hosts)
Initiating Parallel DNS resolution of 1 host. at 16:07
Completed Parallel DNS resolution of 1 host. at 16:08, 16.50s elapsed
Initiating SYN Stealth Scan at 16:08
Scanning 192.168.75.128 [1 port]
Discovered open port 8180/tcp on 192.168.75.128
Completed SYN Stealth Scan at 16:08, 0.00s elapsed (1 total ports)
NSE: Script scanning 192.168.75.128.
Initiating NSE at 16:08
Completed NSE at 16:08, 0.01s elapsed
Nmap scan report for 192.168.75.128
Host is up (0.00088s latency).

PORT     STATE SERVICE
8180/tcp open  unknown
|_apache-default-files: vulnerable
MAC Address: 00:0C:29:74:1C:63 (VMware)

NSE: Script Post-scanning.
Initiating NSE at 16:08
Completed NSE at 16:08, 0.00s elapsed
Read data files from: C:\Program Files (x86)\Nmap
Nmap done: 1 IP address (1 host up) scanned in 33.60 seconds
          Raw packets sent: 2 (72B) | Rcvd: 2 (72B)
```

How it works...

You can use similar techniques to create complex scripts by using complex libraries and using multiple functions of the Lua language, which supports complex programming. These scripts can be executed together based on the port and service available by using the –A argument. This will reduce the effort of the user in terms of mentioning each and every script that's required.

Understanding the Nessus Audit policy and its customization

The Nessus Audit files consist of custom XML-based rules which are needed to perform configuration audit for various platforms. These files allow the user to perform value and regex-based comparisons of the current configuration and determine the gaps present. In general, it is expected that these audit files are prepared in line with the industry standard baselines so that the actual compliance gaps are shown and the administration team can work on hardening and compliance at the same time. A custom audit file is to be saved with the extension .audit.

The following is a generic syntax of a check in the audit files:

```
<item>
 name                        :  " "
 description          :    " "
 info                        :  " "
 value                       :  " "
</item>
```

We will look at some of the standard checks for windows so that we can learn about various generic and custom checks. All the default checks start with `<item>` and all the custom checks start with `<custom_item>`:

- **Value data**: The keywords in the audit file can be assigned data based on the `value_data` tag. This section describes the different keywords which can be defined in the audit file and the values they can hold. The datatype of `value_data` is DWORD. `value_data` can also be fed with complex expressions using arithmetic symbols such as `||`, `&&`, and so on:

  - `Check_type`: This attribute is used to compare whether the value fetched from the remote host is the policy value and returns the result based on the attribute configured. Some of the versions of this attribute are as follows:

    - `CHECK_EQUAL`

    - `CHECK_EQUAL_ANY`

    - `CHECK_NOT_EQUAL`

    - `CHECK_GREATER_THAN`

    - `CHECK_GREATER_THAN_OR_EQUAL`

  - **Info**: This is an optional field which is used to add information about the check being performed. The syntax for this is as follows:

    ```
    info: "Password policy check"
    ```

  - **Debug**: This keyword can be used to obtain information to troubleshoot a check. This generates step-by-step data on the execution of the check, allowing the author to understand the errors.

- **Access Control List Format (ACL)**: This section of the settings contains keywords which can hold values to detect whether the required ACL settings have been applied on the files. The ACL format supports six different types of access list keywords, as follows:
  - File access control checks (`file_acl`)
  - Registry access control checks (`registry_acl`)
  - Service access control checks (`service_acl`)
  - Launch permission control checks (`launch_acl`)
  - Access permission control checks (`access_acl`)

The preceding keywords can be used to define file permissions for a specific user in the following associated types. These categories of permissions might have different changes for different keywords:

- `Acl_inheritance`
- `Acl_apply`
- `Acl_allow`
- `Acl_deny`

These keywords have different sets of permissions for folders. The following is the syntax in which `file_acl` can be used:

```
<file_acl: ["name"]>
<user: ["user_name"]>
acl_inheritance: ["value"]
acl_apply: ["value"]
</user>
</acl>
```

A similar syntax can be used for all the other keywords by just replacing `file_acl` with the respective keyword.

- **Item:** An item is of the check type, and can be used to perform predefined audit checks. This reduces the syntax as the policy is predefined and is called here using the attributes. The following is the structure of an item:

```
<item>
name: ["predefined_entry"]
value: [value]
</item>
```

The value can be defined by the user, but the name needs to match the name which is listed in the predefined policies. The following are a few of the keywords and tags we will use in this recipe to create a custom Windows and Unix audit file.

- `check_type`: Each audit file begins with the `check_type` tag, where the operating system and the version can be defined. This tag needs to be closed once the audit file is complete to mark the end of the audit file:

```
<check_type:"Windows" version:" ">
```

- `name`: The `name` attribute needs to be the same as in the predefined policies in order for the logic to be fetched from the predefined policies:

```
name: "max_password_age"
```

- `type`: The type variable holds the name of the policy item which is used for a specific check:

```
type: PASSWORD_POLICY
```

- `description`: This attribute holds the user-defined name for the check. This can be anything that is useful to identify the action that is going on in the check:

```
description: " Maximum password age"
```

- `info`: This attribute is generally used to hold the logic in order for a user to understand the action being performed in the check:

```
info: "Maximum password age of 60 days is being checked."
```

- `Value`: This attribute is of the DWORD type and consists of the policy value against which the remote value present on the host is to be compared with:

```
Value: "8"
```

- cmd: This holds the command which is to be executed on the remote system in order to obtain the value of the item being checked:

```
cmd : "cat /etc/login.defs | grep -v ^# | grep
PASS_WARN_AGE | awk {'print $2'}"
```

- regex: This attribute can be used to perform regular expression-based comparisons for the remote value obtained. This can then be compared with the policy value to ensure that the check was successful, even if the configuration is stored in a different format:

```
regex: "^[\\s]*PASS_WARN_AGE\\s+"
```

- expect: This policy item consists of the baseline policy value which is expected to be configured on the device. Otherwise, it is used to report the gap in the configuration:

```
expect: "14"
```

- Custom_item: A custom audit check is something that is defined by the user using NASL and is parsed by the Nessus compliance parser as per the instructions provided in the checks. These custom items consist of custom attributes and custom data values, which will allow the user to define the required policy values and prepare the audit files accordingly.

- value_type: This attribute consists of different types of the values which are allowed for the current check:

```
value_type: POLICY_TEXT
```

- value_data: This attribute consists of the types of data that can be entered for the checks, such as:
    - value_data: 0
    - value_data: [0..20]
    - value_data: [0..MAX]

- Powershell_args: This attribute consists of arguments which are to be passed and executed on powershell.exe for a windows system.

- `Ps_encoded_args`: This attribute is used to allow PowerShell arguments or files as base 64 strings to PowerShell, for example, `powershell_args`:

'DQAKACIAMQAwACADFSIGHSAPFIUGHPSAIUFHVPSAIUVHAIPUVAPAUIVHAP
IVdAA7AA0ACgA='
`ps_encoded_args: YES`

In this recipe, we will look at creating a windows audit file to check free disk space in the system partition.

Getting ready

In order to complete this activity, you will have to satisfy the following prerequisites on your machine:

- You must have Nessus installed.
- You must have network access to the hosts on which the scans are to be performed.

In order to install Nessus, you can follow the instructions provided in Chapter 2, *Understanding Network Scanning Tools*. This will allow you to download a compatible version of Nessus and install all the required plugins. In order to check whether your machine has Nessus installed, open the search bar and search for Nessus Web Client. Once found and clicked on, this will be opened in the default browser window:

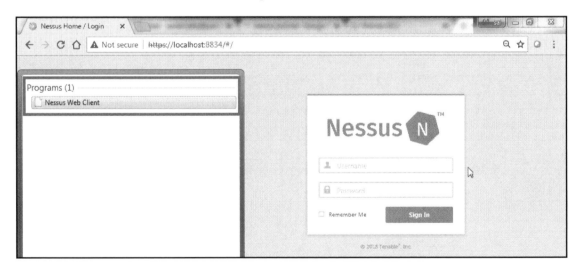

If you are sure that Nessus has been installed correctly, you can use the `https://localhost:8834` URL directly from your browser to open the Nessus Web Client. If you are unable to locate the Nessus Web Client, you should remove and reinstall Nessus. For the removal of Nessus and installation instructions, refer to `Chapter 2`, *Understanding Network Scanning Tools*. If you have located the Nessus Web Client and are unable to open it in the browser window, you need to check whether the Nessus service is running in the Windows Services utility:

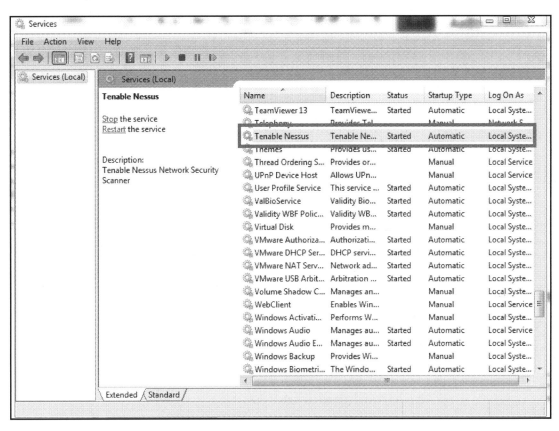

You can further start and stop Nessus by using the **Services** utility as per your requirements. In order to further confirm the installation using the command-line interface, you can navigate to the installation directory to see and access Nessus command-line utilities:

```
C:\Windows\system32\cmd.exe

C:\>cd "Program Files"

C:\Program Files>cd Tenable

C:\Program Files\Tenable>cd Nessus

C:\Program Files\Tenable\Nessus>dir
 Volume in drive C has no label.
 Volume Serial Number is B234-0E80

 Directory of C:\Program Files\Tenable\Nessus

16-07-2018  11:45    <DIR>          .
16-07-2018  11:45    <DIR>          ..
16-07-2018  11:45                 1 .winperms
19-06-2018  17:25            45,113 License.rtf
19-06-2018  19:25         6,459,904 nasl.exe
19-06-2018  19:25            46,592 ndbg.exe
19-06-2018  17:25                46 Nessus Web Client.url
19-06-2018  19:22            17,424 nessus-service.exe
19-06-2018  19:25         6,405,120 nessuscli.exe
19-06-2018  19:25         6,837,776 nessusd.exe
               8 File(s)     19,811,976 bytes
               2 Dir(s)   1,970,270,208 bytes free

C:\Program Files\Tenable\Nessus>
```

It is always recommended to have administrator-level or root-level credentials to provide the scanner access to all the system files. This will allow the scanner to perform a deeper scan and populate better results compared to a non-credentialed scan. The policy compliance module is only available in the paid versions of Nessus, such as Nessus Professional or Nessus Manager. For this, you will have to purchase an activation key from Tenable and update it in the **Settings** page, as shown in the following screenshot:

Click on the edit button to open a window and enter the new activation code you have purchased from Tenable:

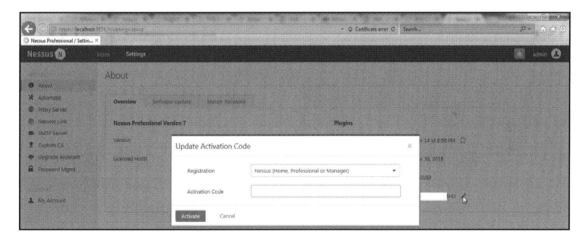

How do it...

Perform the following steps:

1. Open Notepad++ or any text editor.
2. In order to create a Windows check for a custom item, we need to begin and end the check with the `custom_item` tag:

```
<custom_item>



</custom_item>
```

3. Now, we need to identify the required metadata attributes and define them. In this case, we will go with `description` and `info`:

```
<custom_item>


 description: "Free disk space in system partition#C drive"
 info: "Powershell command will output the free space available on
C drive"


</custom_item>
```

4. Now, we need to define the type of check we need to perform. Nessus executes all the NASL windows commands on PowerShell, and so the type of the check would be `AUDIT_POWERSHELL`:

```
<custom_item>


type: AUDIT_POWERSHELL
 description: "Free disk space in system partition#C drive"
 info      : "Powershell command will output the free space
available on C drive"


</custom_item>
```

5. Now, we need to define the value type and value data, which are supported by the check. In this case, we will go with policy type and set `0` to `MAX`:

```
<custom_item>
```

```
type: AUDIT_POWERSHELL
 description: "Free disk space in system partition#C drive"
 info      : "Powershell command will output the free space
available on C drive"
 value_type: POLICY_TEXT
 value_data: "[0..MAX]"



</custom_item>
```

6. Now, we need to pass the command to be executed by PowerShell to obtain free space in the C drive:

```
<custom_item>


 type: AUDIT_POWERSHELL
 description: "Free disk space in system partition#C drive"
 info      : "Powershell command will output the free space
available on C drive"
 value_type: POLICY_TEXT
 value_data: "[0..MAX]"
 powershell_args   : 'Get-PSDrive C | Select-Object Free'


</custom_item>
```

7. As we are not passing encoded commands to PowerShell, we need to define the same with the ps_encoded_args attribute:

```
<custom_item>


 type: AUDIT_POWERSHELL
 description: "Free disk space in system partition#C drive"
 info      : "Powershell command will output the free space
available on C drive"
 value_type: POLICY_TEXT
 value_data: "[0..MAX]"
 powershell_args   : 'Get-PSDrive C | Select-Object Free'
 ps_encoded_args: NO


</custom_item>
```

8. As it does not require any refining and the output of the command will suffice so that we know how much free space we have, we will also define the `only_show_cmd_output: YES` attribute:

```
<custom_item>


 type: AUDIT_POWERSHELL
 description: "Free disk space in system partition#C drive"
 info       : "Powershell command will output the free space
available on C drive"
 value_type: POLICY_TEXT
 value_data: "[0..MAX]"
 powershell_args   : 'Get-PSDrive C | Select-Object Free'
 ps_encoded_args: NO
 only_show_cmd_output: YES


</custom_item>
```

As we have seen that all the audit files start and end with `check_type`, we enclose the preceding code in the same:

```
<check_type:"windows" version:"2">
<custom_item>


 type: AUDIT_POWERSHELL
 description: "Free disk space in system partition#C drive"
 info       : "Powershell command will output the free space
available on C drive"
 value_type: POLICY_TEXT
 value_data: "[0..MAX]"
 powershell_args   : 'Get-PSDrive C | Select-Object Free'
 ps_encoded_args: NO
 only_show_cmd_output: YES


</custom_item>
</check_type>
```

9. Save the file with the extension `.audit` onto your system and log in to Nessus using the credentials created during installation:

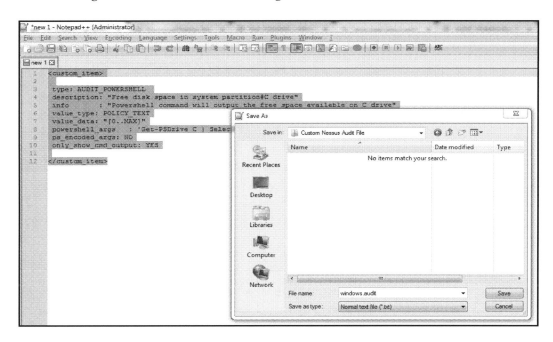

10. Open the **Policy** tab and click on **Create new policy using advanced scan template**. Fill in the required details such as the policy name and description:

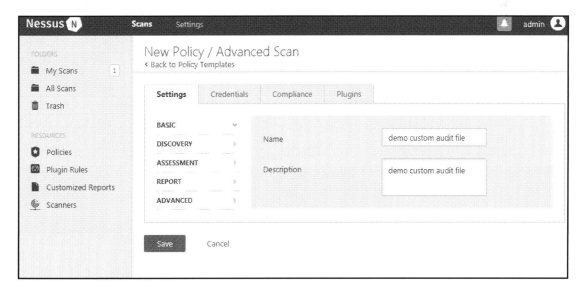

11. Navigate to the **Compliance** section and search the custom windows in the filter compliance search bar:

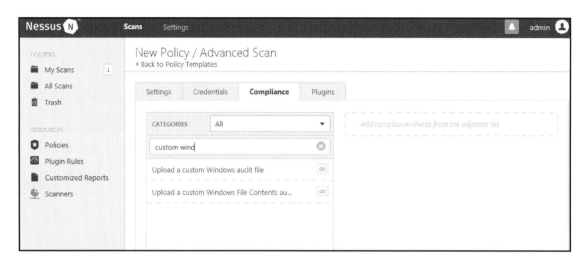

12. Select the **Upload a custom Windows audit file** option:

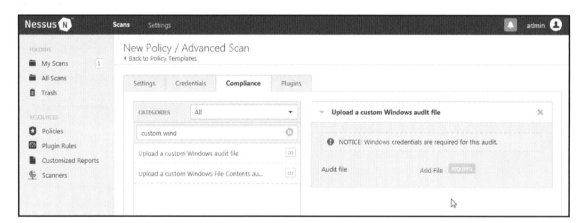

13. Click on **Add File** and upload the audit file you have created:

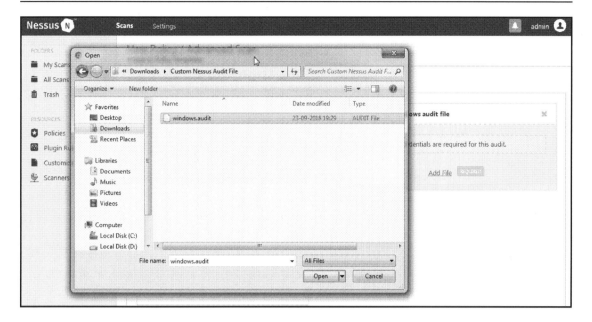

14. In order to perform a compliance audit, you will have to enter the Windows credentials. Navigate to the credentials section and click on the **Windows** option:

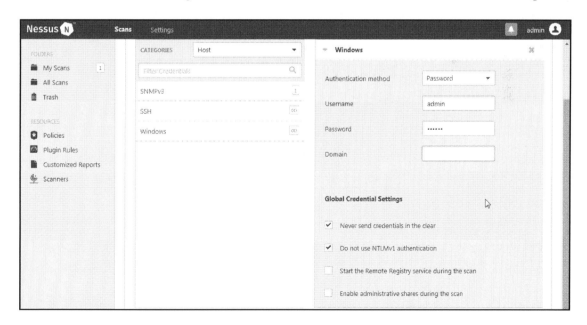

15. Save the policy and navigate to the **My scans** page to create a new scan.

16. Navigate to the **User Defined** policy section and select the custom Windows audit policy that we created:

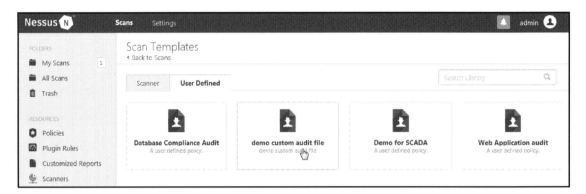

17. Fill in the required details such as the scan name and affected host, and launch the scan:

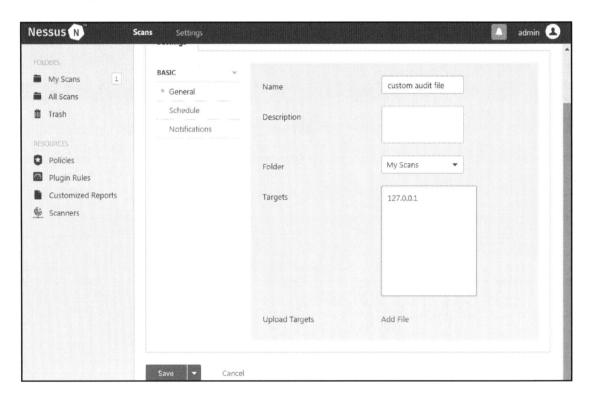

How it works...

These custom audit files can be used to audit multiple platforms, as NASL supports key works and attributes for multiple platforms and these values are custom and specific to the configuration of these platforms. This allows the user to easily create audit files and customize them as per their requirements and their baselines to perform the configuration audit and identify these gaps. The following is a list of platforms supported by Nessus to perform a configuration audit:

- Windows:
    - Windows 2003 Server
    - Windows 2008 Server
    - Windows Vista
    - Windows 7
- Unix:
    - Solaris
    - Linux
    - FreeBSD/OpenBSD/NetBSD
    - HP/UX
    - AIX
    - macOS X
- Other platforms:
    - Cisco
    - SCADA

8
Network Scanning for IoT, SCADA/ICS

In this chapter, we will cover the following recipes:

- Introduction to SCADA/ICS
- Using Nmap to scan SCADA/ICS
- Using Nessus to scan SCADA/ICS systems

Introduction to SCADA/ICS

The automation technology used to manage and perform various industrial operations such as line management control and operations control are part of what is known as operational technology:

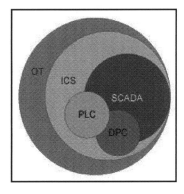

Industrial control systems (ICS) cover a huge part of the operational technology segment, and are used to monitor and control various operations such as automating production, the control and monitoring of hardware systems, regulating temperature by controlling water levels, and the flow at a nuclear facility. Most ICS usage is done in very critical systems that are required to be available all the time.

The hardware that is used for ICS is of two types, **programmable logic controllers (PLCs)**, or **discrete process control systems (DPC)**, which are in turn managed by **Supervisory Control and Data Acquisition (SCADA)** systems. SCADA allows and makes easy the management of ICS systems by providing interface-based control rather than the user having to manually enter each and every command. This makes the management of these systems robust and easy, thereby allowing for a very high availability:

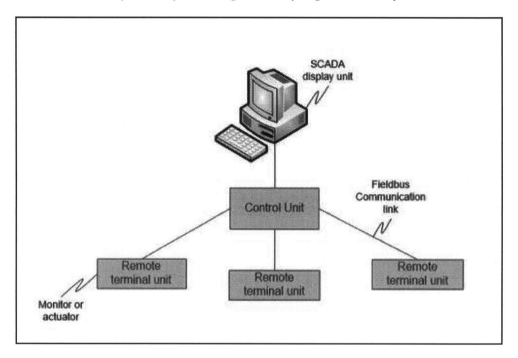

The main components are as follows:

- The SCADA display unit is basically the component that holds an interactive interface for the administrator to review, verify, and modify various commands that are to be passed to the ICS systems. This allows the user to control the ICS system from a distance without actually being in the field. For example, a remote administrator can use a web portal to manage configurations of all the thermostats in a building.

- The control unit acts as a bridge between the SCADA display unit and the remote terminal unit. It is always required for the control unit to send the data coming from remote terminal units to the SCADA display units in real time. This is required in order to notify the administrator of any malfunctions which can be looked at and fixed to ensure the high availability of the system.

- **Remote terminal units** (**RTUs**) can be a **PLC** (a Programmable Logic Controller, which is a manufacturing industry standard computer that is used in manufacturing to process and execute instructions), which connects multiple devices to the SCADA network, enabling them to be monitored and administered from great distances. These links between the RT, the control unit, and the SCADA display unit don't need be in the form of a wired network – it can also be a wireless network.

It is very important to secure these SCADA systems, as a simple misconfiguration could lead to a catastrophe in an actual industrial manufacturing environment. There are many open source tools that can be used for this purpose. Nmap is one such tool that allows users to write custom scripts for SCADA/ICS system port scanning. Furthermore, an analyst can use Metasploit modules to exploit these vulnerabilities in a SCADA/ICS environment.

The following are some of the Metasploit modules that can be used to identify and exploit issues on the SCADA/ICS systems:

Vendor	System/component	Metasploit module
7-Technologies	IGSS	`exploit/windows/scada/igss9_igssdataserver_listall.rb`
		`exploit/windows/scada/igss9_igssdataserver_rename.rb`
		`exploit/windows/scada/igss9_misc.rb`
		`auxiliary/admin/scada/igss_exec_17.rb`
AzeoTech	DAQ Factory	`exploit/windows/scada/daq_factory_bof.rb`
3S	CoDeSys	`exploit/windows/scada/codesys_web_server.rb`
BACnet	OPC Client	`exploit/windows/fileformat/bacnet_csv.rb`
	Operator Workstation	`exploit/windows/browser/teechart_pro.rb`
Beckhoff	TwinCat	`auxiliary/dos/scada/beckhoff_twincat.rb`
General Electric	D20 PLC	`auxiliary/gather/d20pass.rb`
		`unstable-modules/auxiliary/d20tftpbd.rb`
Iconics	Genesis32	`exploit/windows/scada/iconics_genbroker.rb`
		`exploit/windows/scada/iconics_webhmi_setactivexguid.rb`
Measuresoft	ScadaPro	`exploit/windows/scada/scadapro_cmdexe.rb`
Moxa	Device Manager	`exploit/windows/scada/moxa_mdmtool.rb`
RealFlex	RealWin SCADA	`exploit/windows/scada/realwin.rb`

		`exploit/windows/scada/realwin_scpc_initialize.rb`
		`exploit/windows/scada/realwin_scpc_initialize_rf.rb`
		`exploit/windows/scada/realwin_scpc_txtevent.rb`
		`exploit/windows/scada/realwin_on_fc_binfile_a.rb`
		`exploit/windows/scada/realwin_on_fcs_login.rb`
Scadatec	Procyon	`exploit/windows/scada/procyon_core_server.rb`
Schneider Electric	CitectSCADA	`exploit/windows/scada/citect_scada_odbc.rb`
SielcoSistemi	Winlog	`exploit/windows/scada/winlog_runtime.rb`
Siemens Technomatix	FactoryLink	`exploit/windows/scada/factorylink_cssservice.rb`
		`exploit/windows/scada/factorylink_vrn_09.rb`
Unitronics	OPC Server	`exploit/exploits/windows/browser/teechart_pro.rb`

There are many open source tools as well that can be used to perform these operations. One such tool is PLCScan.

PLCScan is a utility that's used to identify PLC devices using port scanning methodology. This identifies the packets received from specific ports to specific signatures of various SCADA/PLC devices that have been previously documented. It uses a set of scripts in the backend to perform these operations.

Scanning a control system by using automation scripts could be a tedious task, as they can crash very easily. Most of the SCADA/ICS systems are legacy systems with legacy software, which are not very cost-effective for replacement and do not have enough hardware to be automated. This results in a lot of vulnerabilities.

Using Nmap to scan SCADA/ICS

Nmap provides multiple scripts, and its function also allows users to create multiple custom scripts to identify the SCADA systems that are present in a network. This allows an analyst to create specific test cases to test the SCADA systems. Some of the scripts that are available by default in the latest Nmap Script library are as follows:

- `s7-info.nse`: This is used to enumerate Siemens S7 PLC devices and collect information such as system name, version, module, and type. This script works similarly to that of the PLCScan utility.
- `modbus-discover.nse`: Enumerates SCADA Modbus **slave ids** (**sids**) and collects information such as sid number and slave ID data. Modbus is a protocol used by various PLC and SCADA systems.

We will see the syntax and the usage of these scripts in the following recipes.

Getting ready

In order to complete this activity, you will have to satisfy the following prerequisites on your machine:

1. You must have Nmap installed.
2. You must have network access to the hosts on which the scans are to be performed.

In order to install Nmap, you can follow the instructions provided in Chapter 2, *Understanding Network Scanning Tools*. This will allow you to download a compatible version of Nmap and install all the required plugins. In order to check whether your machine has Nmap installed, open Command Prompt and type Nmap. If Nmap is installed, you will see a screen similar to the following:

```
C:\Windows\system32\cmd.exe

Microsoft Windows [Version 6.1.7601]
Copyright (c) 2009 Microsoft Corporation.  All rights reserved.

C:\Users\admin>nmap
Nmap 7.70 ( https://nmap.org )
Usage: nmap [Scan Type(s)] [Options] {target specification}
TARGET SPECIFICATION:
  Can pass hostnames, IP addresses, networks, etc.
  Ex: scanme.nmap.org, microsoft.com/24, 192.168.0.1; 10.0.0-255.1-254
  -iL <inputfilename>: Input from list of hosts/networks
  -iR <num hosts>: Choose random targets
  --exclude <host1[,host2][,host3],...>: Exclude hosts/networks
  --excludefile <exclude_file>: Exclude list from file
HOST DISCOVERY:
  -sL: List Scan - simply list targets to scan
  -sn: Ping Scan - disable port scan
  -Pn: Treat all hosts as online -- skip host discovery
  -PS/PA/PU/PY[portlist]: TCP SYN/ACK, UDP or SCTP discovery to given ports
  -PE/PP/PM: ICMP echo, timestamp, and netmask request discovery probes
  -PO[protocol list]: IP Protocol Ping
  -n/-R: Never do DNS resolution/Always resolve [default: sometimes]
  --dns-servers <serv1[,serv2],...>: Specify custom DNS servers
  --system-dns: Use OS's DNS resolver
  --traceroute: Trace hop path to each host
SCAN TECHNIQUES:
  -sS/sT/sA/sW/sM: TCP SYN/Connect()/ACK/Window/Maimon scans
  -sU: UDP Scan
  -sN/sF/sX: TCP Null, FIN, and Xmas scans
  --scanflags <flags>: Customize TCP scan flags
```

If you do not see the preceding screen, retry the same step by moving the Command Prompt control into the folder where Nmap is installed (C:\Program Files\Nmap). If you do not see the screen after doing this, remove and reinstall Nmap.

To populate the open ports on hosts for which the scan is to be done on, you are required to have network-level access to that particular host. A simple way to check whether you have access to a particular host is through ICMP by sending ping packets to the host. However, this method only works if ICMP and ping is enabled in that network. In cases where ICMP is disabled, live host detection techniques vary. We will look at this in detail in further sections of this book.

Furthermore, to create a test bed, install Conpot, which is a well-known honey pot on Kali operating systems, by following the instructions provided at https://github.com/mushorg/conpot.

Once Conpot is installed, run Conpot on the system by using the following command:

```
sudoconpot --template default
```

How do it...

Perform the following steps:

1. Open Nmap in Command Prompt.

2. Enter the following syntax in Command Prompt to obtain the scan results for the `scripts7-info.nse` script:

```
Nmap --script s7-info.nse -p 102 192.168.75.133
```

```
C:\Users\admin>nmap --script s7-info.nse -p 102 192.168.75.133
Starting Nmap 7.70 ( https://nmap.org ) at 2018-09-22 13:15 Arabian Standard Time
Stats: 0:00:05 elapsed; 0 hosts completed (0 up), 1 undergoing ARP Ping Scan
ARP Ping Scan Timing: About 100.00% done; ETC: 13:15 (0:00:00 remaining)
Nmap scan report for 192.168.75.133
Host is up (0.00s latency).

PORT     STATE SERVICE
102/tcp open  iso-tsap
| s7-info:
|   Version: 0.0
|   System Name: Technodrome
|   Module Type: Siemens, SIMATIC, S7-200
|   Serial Number: 88111222
|   Plant Identification: Mouser Factory
|_  Copyright: Original Siemens Equipment
MAC Address: 00:0C:29:74:28:93 (VMware)
Service Info: Device: specialized

Nmap done: 1 IP address (1 host up) scanned in 18.84 seconds

C:\Users\admin>
```

You can observe that the scanner has detected the system as a `Siemens, SIMATIC, S7-200` appliance.

3. Enter the following syntax in Command Prompt to obtain the scan results for the `modbu-discover.nse` script:

```
Nmap --script modbus-discover.nse --script-args='modbus-
discover.aggressive=true' -p 502 192.168.75.133
```

```
C:\Users\admin>nmap --script modbus-discover.nse --script-args='modbus-discover.aggressive=true' -p 502 192.168.75.133
Starting Nmap 7.70 ( https://nmap.org ) at 2018-09-22 13:17 Arabian Standard Time
Nmap scan report for 192.168.75.133
Host is up (0.00s latency).

PORT     STATE SERVICE
502/tcp open  modbus
| modbus-discover:
|   sid 0x1:
|     Slave ID data: <unknown>
|_    Device identification: Siemens SIMATIC S7-200
MAC Address: 00:0C:29:74:28:93 (VMware)

Nmap done: 1 IP address (1 host up) scanned in 17.66 seconds

C:\Users\admin>
```

This module has also discovered the device to be `Siemens, SIMATIC, S7-200`.

How it works...

These Nmap scripts allow the user to identify the specific ports that have been in use by the SCADA systems. For example, as shown in the proceeding recipe, ports 102 and 502 are specific ports that can be used to determine whether there are any SIMATIC devices in the network. An analyst can scan the whole network for ports 102 and 502, and once found, they can perform a service scan to check whether any of them are running any related SCADA software.

There's more...

At any given instance, if the default scripts present in Nmap have not done the job, then the user can download the custom Nmap scripts developed by other developers from GitHub or any resource and paste them into the scripts folder of the Nmap installation folder to use them. For example, clone the folder from the link https://github.com/jpalanco/Nmap-scada for multiple other SCADA systems and paste them in the scripts folder so that you can run them using Nmap:

📄 README.md	Added more checks to CommunicationsProcessor
📄 Siemens-CommunicationsProcessor.nse	Added support for more versions
📄 Siemens-HMI-miniweb.nse	Added more checks to CommunicationsProcessor
📄 Siemens-SIMATIC-PLC-S7.nse	Added support for SCALANCE XF Family
📄 Siemens-Scalance-module.nse	Added Siemens SCALANCE network devices
📄 Siemens-WINCC.nse	Siemens WINCC discovery support added

Using Nessus to scan SCADA/ICS systems

Nessus has a family of plugins – about 308 pages of them – that can be used to perform scans on SCADA/ICS devices. You can browse the family of plugins here: `https://www.`
`tenable.com/plugins/nessus/families/SCADA`. These plugins are checked against the given device to identify any vulnerability that has been identified based on the signatures present in the plugin.

Getting ready

In order to complete this activity, you will have to satisfy the following prerequisites on your machine:

1. You must have Nessus installed.
2. You must have network access to the hosts on which the scans are to be performed.

In order to install Nessus, you can follow the instructions provided in `Chapter 2`, *Understanding Network Scanning Tools*. This will allow you to download a compatible version of Nessus and install all the required plugins. In order to check whether your machine has Nessus installed, open the search bar and search for `Nessus Web Client`. Once found and clicked, this will be opened in the default browser window:

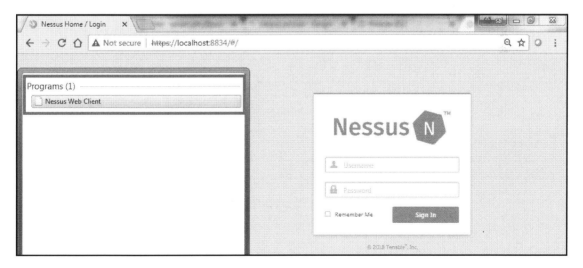

If you are sure that Nessus has been installed correctly, you can use the `https://localhost:8834` URL directly from your browser to open the Nessus Web Client. If you are unable to locate the **Nessus Web Client**, you should remove and reinstall Nessus. For the removal of Nessus and installation instructions, refer to `Chapter 2`, *Understanding Network Scanning Tools*. If you have located the Nessus Web Client and are unable to open it in the browser window, you need to check whether the Nessus service is running in the Windows Services utility:

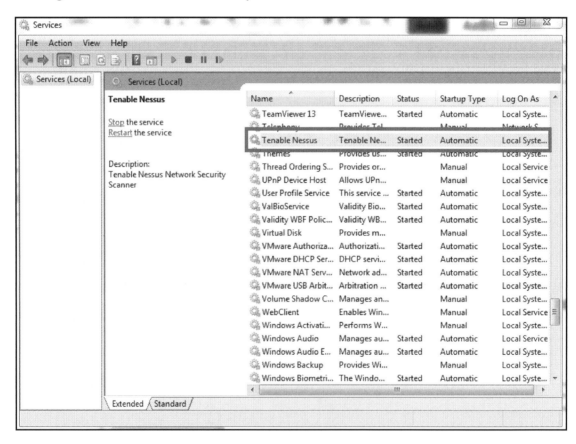

Furthermore, you can start and stop Nessus by using the services utility as per your requirements. In order to further confirm this installation using the command-line interface, you can navigate to the installation directory to see and access Nessus' command-line utilities:

```
C:\Windows\system32\cmd.exe

C:\>cd "Program Files"

C:\Program Files>cd Tenable

C:\Program Files\Tenable>cd Nessus

C:\Program Files\Tenable\Nessus>dir
 Volume in drive C has no label.
 Volume Serial Number is B234-0E80

 Directory of C:\Program Files\Tenable\Nessus

16-07-2018  11:45    <DIR>          .
16-07-2018  11:45    <DIR>          ..
16-07-2018  11:45                 1 .winperms
19-06-2018  17:25            45,113 License.rtf
19-06-2018  19:25         6,459,904 nasl.exe
19-06-2018  19:25            46,592 ndbg.exe
19-06-2018  17:25                46 Nessus Web Client.url
19-06-2018  19:22            17,424 nessus-service.exe
19-06-2018  19:25         6,405,120 nessuscli.exe
19-06-2018  19:25         6,837,776 nessusd.exe
               8 File(s)     19,811,976 bytes
               2 Dir(s)   1,970,270,208 bytes free

C:\Program Files\Tenable\Nessus>
```

It is always recommended to have administrator-level or root-level credentials to provide the scanner with access to all the system files. This will allow the scanner to perform a deeper scan and populate better results compared to a non-credentialed scan. The policy compliance module is only available in the paid version of Nessus, such as Nessus Professional or Nessus Manager. For this, you will have to purchase an activation key from tenable and update it in the settings page, as shown in the following screenshot:

Click on the edit button to open a window and enter the new activation code that you have purchased from tenable:

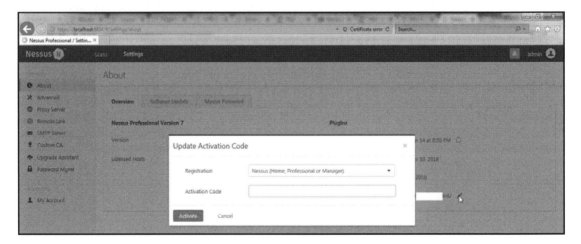

Furthermore, you can install Conpot, as mentioned in the previous recipe. This recipe also requires the installation of the Kali Linux operating system. You can download a virtual machine from `https://www.vmware.com/products/workstation-pro/workstation-pro-evaluation.html` and Kali Linux from `https://www.offensive-security.com/kali-linux-vm-vmware-virtualbox-image-download/`.

How do it..

Perform the following steps:

1. Open the Nessus web client.
2. Log in to the Nessus client with the user that you created during installation.
3. Click on the **Policies** tab and select **Create New Policy**. Then, select the **Basic Network Scan** template:

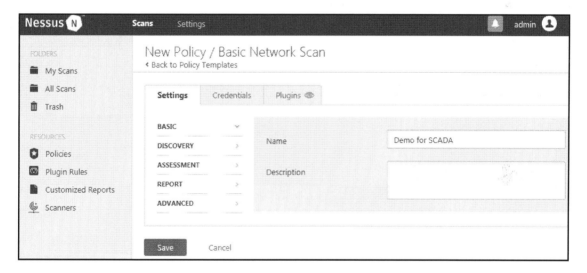

Alter the settings in the **Discovery** tab for the port scan by mentioning a range from 1–1000. This will allow the scanner to complete the scan quickly:

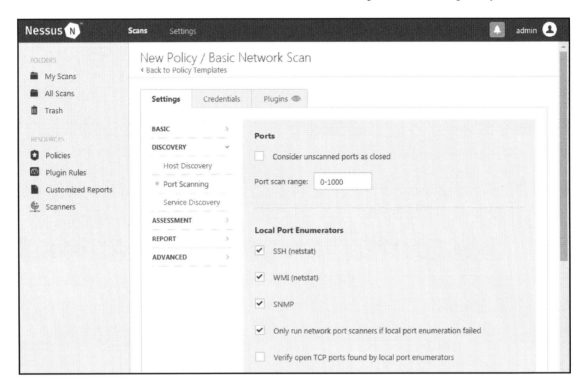

4. Ensure that **Perform thorough tests** is not selected in the accuracy tab of the **General** settings category in **ASSESSMENT**:

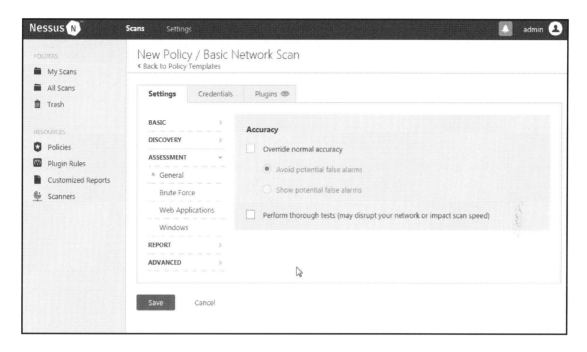

This will ensure that the PLC or any other device on which you are performing the scan is not affected in any way due to the traffic produced. You can also set advanced settings to ensure that minimal traffic is generated:

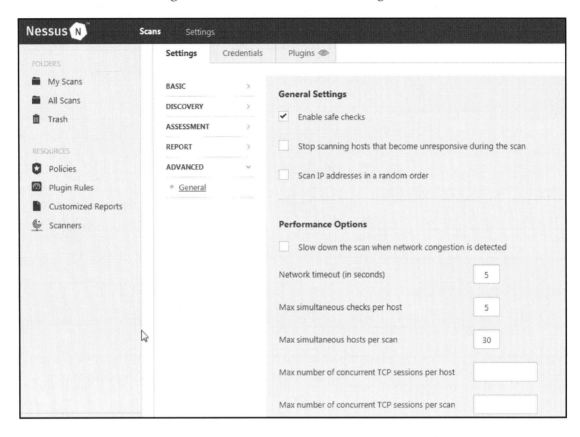

5. Ensure that the SCADA plugins are present in the **Plugins** tab, otherwise the results obtained would only be for non-SCADA ports:

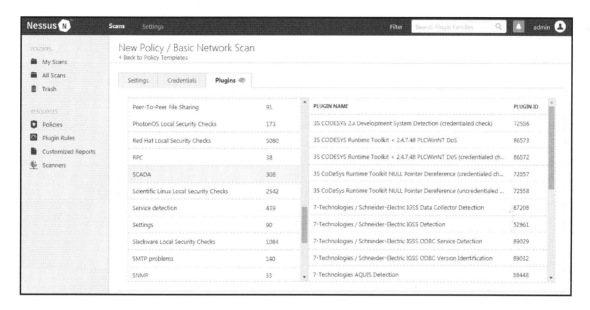

6. Save the policy and select **New Scan** from the `My Scans` folder. Navigate to the **User Defined** policies section and select the policy:

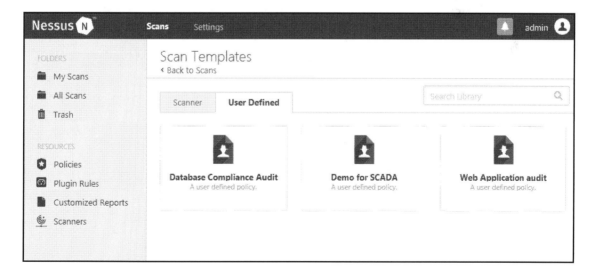

7. Select the policy and fill in the required details. Then, launch the scan:

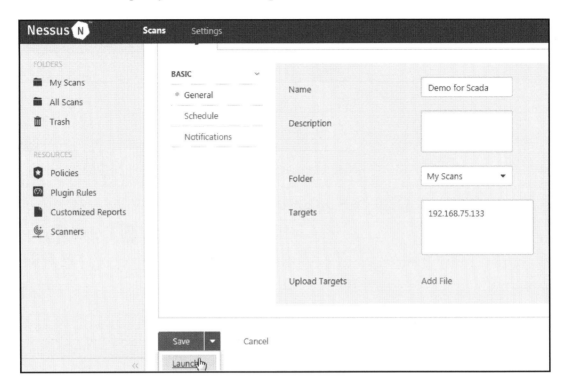

8. Wait for the scan to complete and open the results:

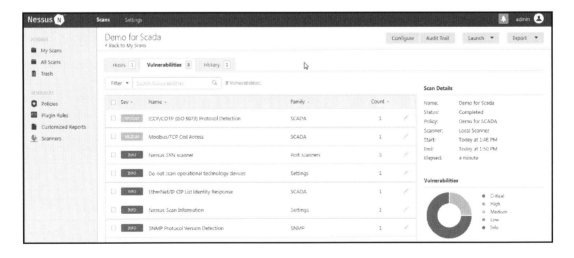

The preceding results show us that the scan was successful and that Nessus has found two SCADA-related vulnerabilities:

- **ICCP/COTP (ISO 8073) Protocol Detection:**

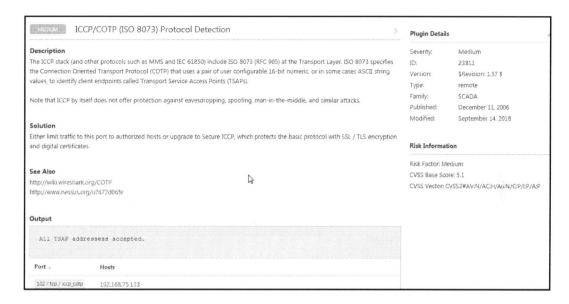

- **Modbus/TCP Coil Access:**

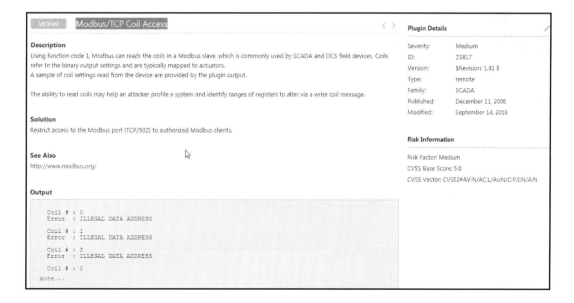

How it works...

These scan results will allow the user to perform further analysis to check for the known vulnerabilities in the system. From this, the user can suggest the required patches to the administrator. It should always be ensured that all the SCADA connections are encrypted and end-to-end, or else restricted only to performing point-to-point connections.

There's more...

Similar checks can be performed using the Metasploit modules. Open Kali Linux, which we installed in the VM, and type the following command in Terminal:

```
msfconsole
```

```
root@kali:~# msfconsole
[-] Failed to connect to the database: could not connect to server: Connection ref
used
        Is the server running on host "localhost" (::1) and accepting
        TCP/IP connections on port 5432?
could not connect to server: Connection refused
        Is the server running on host "localhost" (127.0.0.1) and accepting
        TCP/IP connections on port 5432?




             /                \
      ((_____ ,,,,--- ))
         () o o ()
            \  /              |\
         o_o \   M S F   | \
              \             |  \
              |||  __  |||        *
              |||  WW|||
              |||          |||


        =[ metasploit v4.16.7-dev                        ]
+ -- --=[ 1683 exploits - 964 auxiliary - 299 post    ]
+ -- --=[ 498 payloads - 40 encoders - 10 nops         ]
+ -- --=[ Free Metasploit Pro trial: http://r-7.co/trymsp ]
```

This is used to open the Metasploit console. There is also a GUI version of Metasploit available with the name Armitage. To find out the various Metasploit modules that are available for SCADA, enter the following command:

```
searchscada
```

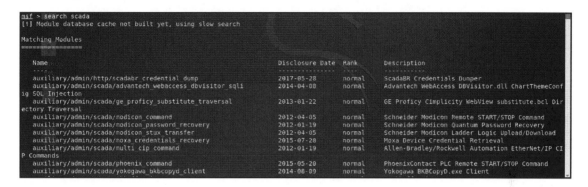

As shown in the preceding screenshot, various modules for SCADA that are supported by Metasploit are loaded. Let's try a specific search for Modbus to see what modules are supported:

```
searchmodbus
```

From the preceding screenshot, you can use `modbusdetect` to identify whether Modbus is running on port `502` using the following syntax:

```
use auxiliary/scanner/scada/modbusdetect
```

Fill in the required details by using `show options` to identify the same:

```
msf > use auxiliary/scanner/scada/modbusdetect
msf auxiliary(modbusdetect) > show options

Module options (auxiliary/scanner/scada/modbusdetect):

   Name      Current Setting  Required  Description
   ----      ---------------  --------  -----------
   RHOSTS                     yes       The target address range or CIDR identifier
   RPORT     502              yes       The target port (TCP)
   THREADS   1                yes       The number of concurrent threads
   TIMEOUT   10               yes       Timeout for the network probe
   UNIT_ID   1                yes       ModBus Unit Identifier, 1..255, most often 1

msf auxiliary(modbusdetect) >
```

Set RHOSTS to `192.168.75.133` using the following command and run the exploit:

```
set RHOSTS 192.168.75.133
```

```
msf auxiliary(modbusdetect) > set RHOSTS 192.168.75.133
RHOSTS => 192.168.75.133
msf auxiliary(modbusdetect) > exploit

[+] 192.168.75.133:502    - 192.168.75.133:502 - MODBUS - received correct MODBUS/TCP header (unit-ID: 1)
[*] Scanned 1 of 1 hosts (100% complete)
[*] Auxiliary module execution completed
msf auxiliary(modbusdetect) >
```

The preceding screenshot shows that the module has detected the presence of Modbus on port 502.

Other Books You May Enjoy

If you enjoyed this book, you may be interested in these other books by Packt:

Practical Network Scanning

Ajay Singh Chauhan

ISBN: 978-1-78883-923-5

- Achieve an effective security posture to design security architectures
- Learn vital security aspects before moving to the Cloud
- Launch secure applications with Web Application Security and SQL Injection
- Explore the basics of threat detection/response/ mitigation with important use cases
- Learn all about integration principles for PKI and tips to secure it
- Design a WAN infrastructure and ensure security over a public WAN

Network Vulnerability Assessment
Sagar Rahalkar

ISBN: 978-1-78862-725-2

- Develop a cost-effective end-to-end vulnerability management program
- Implement a vulnerability management program from a governance perspective
- Learn about various standards and frameworks for vulnerability assessments and penetration testing
- Understand penetration testing with practical learning on various supporting tools and techniques
- Gain insight into vulnerability scoring and reporting
- Explore the importance of patching and security hardening
- Develop metrics to measure the success of the vulnerability management program

Leave a review - let other readers know what you think

Please share your thoughts on this book with others by leaving a review on the site that you bought it from. If you purchased the book from Amazon, please leave us an honest review on this book's Amazon page. This is vital so that other potential readers can see and use your unbiased opinion to make purchasing decisions, we can understand what our customers think about our products, and our authors can see your feedback on the title that they have worked with Packt to create. It will only take a few minutes of your time, but is valuable to other potential customers, our authors, and Packt. Thank you!

Index

Made in the USA
Coppell, TX
05 December 2019